# Birth Chart

## INTERPRETATION

### Plain & Simple

## About the Author

Andrea Taylor (Dorset, England) has been an astrological counselor for over forty years. Originally self-taught, she studied through the Huber School in the mid-1980s and began teaching birth chart interpretation soon after, gaining clients worldwide. Andrea is also the author of *The Astrology Book* (Honeybee Books, 2014).

## To Write to the Author

If you wish to contact the author or would like more information about this book, please write to the author in care of Llewellyn Worldwide Ltd. and we will forward your request. Both the author and publisher appreciate hearing from you and learning of your enjoyment of this book and how it has helped you. Llewellyn Worldwide Ltd. cannot guarantee that every letter written to the author can be answered, but all will be forwarded. Please write to:

Andrea Taylor
℅ Llewellyn Worldwide
2143 Wooddale Drive
Woodbury, MN 55125-2989

Please enclose a self-addressed stamped envelope for reply,
or $1.00 to cover costs. If outside the U.S.A., enclose
an international postal reply coupon.

Many of Llewellyn's authors have websites with additional information and resources. For more information, please visit our website at http://www.llewellyn.com.

# Birth Chart

## INTERPRETATION

## Plain & Simple

## ANDREA TAYLOR

Llewellyn Publications
Woodbury, Minnesota

First Edition
First Printing, 2022

Book design by Samantha Peterson
Cover design by Kevin R. Brown
Interior art by Llewellyn Art Department

Llewellyn Publications is a registered trademark of Llewellyn Worldwide Ltd.

**Library of Congress Cataloging-in-Publication Data**
Names: Taylor, Andrea, author.
Title: Birth chart interpretation plain & simple / Andrea Taylor.
Other titles: Birth chart interpretation plain and simple
Description: First edition. | Woodbury, Minnesota : Llewellyn Publications, 2022. | Summary: "Concise and beginner-friendly, this practical book discusses how the elements of your birth chart work together to create the unique individual you are"— Provided by publisher.
Identifiers: LCCN 2021051313 (print) | LCCN 2021051314 (ebook) | ISBN 9780738769875 | ISBN 9780738770581 (ebook)
Subjects: LCSH: Birth charts. | Natal astrology.
Classification: LCC BF1719 .T39 2022 (print) | LCC BF1719 (ebook) | DDC 133.5—dc23/eng/20211104
LC record available at https://lccn.loc.gov/2021051313
LC ebook record available at https://lccn.loc.gov/2021051314

Llewellyn Worldwide Ltd. does not participate in, endorse, or have any authority or responsibility concerning private business transactions between our authors and the public.

All mail addressed to the author is forwarded but the publisher cannot, unless specifically instructed by the author, give out an address or phone number.

Any internet references contained in this work are current at publication time, but the publisher cannot guarantee that a specific location will continue to be maintained. Please refer to the publisher's website for links to authors' websites and other sources.

Llewellyn Publications
A Division of Llewellyn Worldwide Ltd.
2143 Wooddale Drive
Woodbury, MN 55125-2989
www.llewellyn.com

Printed in the United States of America

## Other Books by Andrea Taylor

*The Astrology Book*
*Clementine and Beech*
*The de Amerley Affair*
*Mrs. Darling's Daughters*
*Northlands*
*The Queen's Protector*
*Sophia*
*Your Baby's Chart*

## Forthcoming Books by Andrea Taylor

*What's Your Big Three?*

*This book is dedicated to Alina, my dear friend and Aries soul sister, who suggested I write this and with whom I've spent many a happy hour discussing astrological psychology.*

# CONTENTS

# INTRODUCTION

**S**uccinct but with nothing left undone, this book will teach you how to interpret a birth chart. Forty years of teaching and counselling have perfected my method. Combining traditional knowledge with a more modern psychological approach provides an accurate and enlightening chart interpretation relevant to today's world. Take each chapter slowly, absorb the information, work through your own chart step-by-step, and by the end of this book you should be able to successfully read a birth chart.

There is a mystique surrounding all things esoteric, yet astrology is a science based on thousands of years of research. Pare it down and you are left with some pretty basic stuff. And that is what I present in this book: the very basics of interpreting a chart, a course for those who are interested in astrology but who don't have years to devote to research or expensive classes.

A birth chart is a picture of the heavens the moment you were born and drew your first breath. The sky above is full of stars and planets, but a birth chart concentrates only on those planets close enough to exert their influence upon a person. Hence, there are ten planets that are important in a birth chart. No one really understands why these planet energies connect us or why these planets have such a powerful impact on people, but one only has to analyse the moon's sway over Earth's tides to realise there are unseen forces yet to be defined by physicists.

Each of the ten planets has their own energy and reflects different facets of your personality. Most beginning astrologers know about how the sun and the moon affect a birth chart, but what about Mercury, Venus, Mars, Jupiter, Saturn, Uranus, Neptune, and Pluto? They each have a role to play in a chart, defining and describing who you are and how you act.

The following chapters will take you through all you need to know to begin interpreting birth charts. You will learn about the twelve astrological signs, the ten important planets, and the twelve houses. You will also learn how to understand elements and motivations, what the quadrants can teach about people's hidden impulses, and how planets work on angles. You'll discover what faraway Uranus, Neptune, and Pluto mean in a birth chart and how important they are, and you'll learn what happens when planets are grouped together (called a *conjunction*). You will find out what those coloured lines and patterns (also known as *aspects*) in the centre of a birth chart mean, and you'll also learn all about Saturn, whose position in a birth chart describes karmic lessons. And, even more importantly, we'll discuss the north and south nodes. The nodes are a guide to the life path a person is meant to follow in order to bring enlightenment and fulfilment. By the end of this book, you will be well-equipped to interpret your birth chart—as well as anyone else's!

In today's day and age, we are fortunate to be able to computer-generate a birth chart. A fair competence with math was required to generate a birth chart when I started out forty years ago, but now it's easy to generate a chart for free on the internet. Visit a birth chart website and enter your date, time, and place of birth. Your time of birth is very important. If it isn't accurate, your chart won't be. It is usually marked on your birth certificate, but older family members may be able to help.

When creating your birth chart, I advise choosing a Huber chart. There is a place on most sites where you can select which house system you want; click on Huber. While I have no problem with any of the other house systems, a Huber chart is the easiest to use and interpret, and this book is using that chart system. Then print out your chart or save the image on your computer or phone. Once your birth chart is in front of you, you are ready to begin!

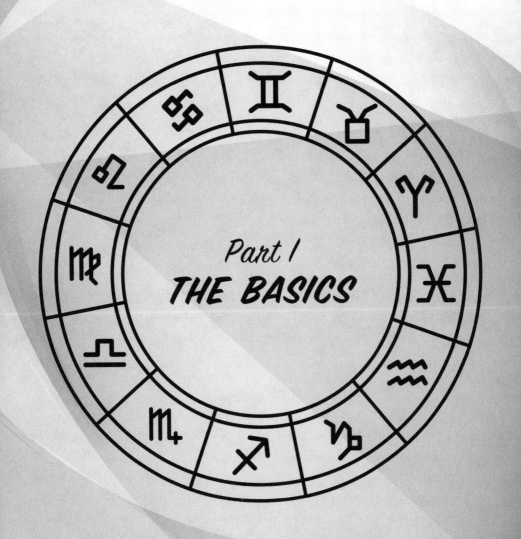

Part 1
THE BASICS

# *One*
# THE ASTROLOGICAL SIGNS AND THEIR ELEMENTS

*W*hen ancient astrologers mapped out the skies, they used the constella-
tions to divide the heavens into the twelve areas we know today as the
astrological signs. Before we learn what it means to have the sun in these
signs, we need to understand each sign's individual energies. To do this, you
only have to learn two things: whether the astrological sign is fire, earth, air,
or water and whether it is cardinal, fixed, or mutable.

## The Elements

Let's look at the elements first: fire, earth, air, and water.

### Fire Signs

The element of fire means action and optimism. Fire signs initiate and act.
They are adventure-seeking and require independence. The three fire signs
all have these traits. Think of colour; red correlates with fire, so fire signs are
red signs. The colour red signifies danger and daring. This is the easiest way
to recall how these planets work. The fire signs are Aries, Leo, and Sagittarius.

## Earth Signs

The earth element means stability and the need for security, continuity, and safety. The three earth signs have these traits. They do not like change and cling to what makes them feel secure, be it a job, people, or places. They build on firm foundations and like to see tangible results from their efforts. Think of earth signs as the colour green. Like the earth itself, they change little and do so slowly. With earth signs, things take time. The three earth signs are Taurus, Virgo, and Capricorn.

## Air Signs

Air signs are the thinkers. They analyse, discuss, exchange information, write, read, and teach. The three air signs have these traits. The mind is more important to them than the body. Relationships are about connecting on a mental level—the physical is less important. Think of air signs as the colour yellow. The air signs are Gemini, Libra, and Aquarius.

## Water Signs

Water signs are the most emotional and sensitive. Instinct, passion, and gut feelings guide them. Everything they do in life is based on how they feel about something. Their decisions are emotional and not always logical. Think of water signs as the colour blue. The water signs are Cancer, Scorpio, and Pisces.

☽ ✳ ☾

Pull up your birth chart and look for the sun symbol. It is drawn as a circle with a dot in the middle. What astrological sign is your sun in?

Remembering what you have just learnt, can you see how the element the sun is in reflects your personality? Try to always remember the element a sun sign is because this will help you recall how it acts.

# The Motivations

Moving on, each astrological sign is also cardinal, fixed, or mutable.

## Cardinal Signs

There will be one sign from each element (fire, earth, air, and water) that is cardinal. The cardinal signs are Aries, Capricorn, Libra, and Cancer.

Cardinal signs are capable of leadership and independent action. They do not need to be part of a group to act, nor do they need the support of others to do so. They cope with the difficulties of life by picking themselves up, dusting themselves off, and starting over again. They like to initiate projects. Cardinal signs are proactive.

## Fixed Signs

There will be one sign from each element (fire, earth, air, and water) that is fixed. The fixed signs are Leo, Taurus, Aquarius, and Scorpio.

These four signs all need stability in life. Once decisions have been made, they do not like change. They like to stay put in jobs and relationships. Once they have set their sights on something, be it a partner or a job, they allow nothing to deflect them from their goal. Once they have what they are after, no one can make them move on until they choose to do so. People who try to push a fixed sign will fail.

## Mutable Signs

There will be one sign from each element (fire, earth, air, and water) that is mutable. The mutable signs are Sagittarius, Virgo, Gemini, and Pisces.

Mutable means changeable. These four signs adapt well to change and are flexible in thought and deed. They easily cope with changing circumstances. They can handle whatever life throws at them.

☽ ✳ ☾

All books with written descriptions of sun signs are only using this basic knowledge and applying it to different situations. There is no need to learn huge swathes of descriptions of sun signs. Just remember what element a sign is (fire, earth, air, or water) and its motivation (cardinal, fixed, or mutable) and you can accurately predict how a person with that sun sign will act in any situation.

What is your sun sign's motivation? Are you cardinal, fixed, or mutable? Can you relate to this?

## Element and Motivation Count

Before we move on to the next section, look again at your birth chart and count how many planets are in each element. In other words, how many of the planet symbols (there will be eleven) are in fire, earth, air, and water signs? Which element do you have the most of in your chart? Make a note.

Now count how many of your planets are in cardinal, fixed, and mutable signs. Which quality do you have the most of?

Put the elements and motivations together to see which astrological sign traits you inherited at birth. For example, if the majority of your planetary elements are earth and you have a high number of mutable planetary motivations, you probably have a lot in common with Virgos, even if that is not your sun sign.

Remember:

- Aries is cardinal fire.
- Taurus is fixed earth.
- Gemini is mutable air.
- Cancer is cardinal water.
- Leo is fixed fire.
- Virgo is mutable earth.
- Libra is cardinal air.
- Scorpio is fixed water.
- Sagittarius is mutable fire.
- Capricorn is cardinal earth.
- Aquarius is fixed air.
- Pisces is mutable water.

Keep this information handy because we will come back to it later.

☽ ✳ ☾

Now that you know the basics, let's discuss each astrological sign.

The sun is the most important planet in a birth chart. The astrological sign it is in at your birth describes your most obvious characteristics, the traits you must outwardly express to be true to yourself. It is how you display your identity and individuality.

The earth takes one year to make its entire rotation of the sun. Because of this guaranteed accuracy, the sun is the only planet that can be assigned concrete dates as to where it will be throughout the year. This is why it is the facet of a birth chart that most people are familiar with. But although sun signs have pretty specific dates, sometimes even they change by a day or two. This is because the sky is a circle of 360 degrees, but there are 365 days in a year. That's why we have an extra day in our calendar every four years and why sun sign dates are slightly fluid—and why your time of birth is the only accurate guide to which sun sign you are. The other planets move more irregularly and erratically. Some planets move fast, like the moon, which passes through each astrological sign every two and a half days. Others, like Pluto, move slowly. Pluto, which is the planet in a birth chart that is farthest away from Earth, takes 248 years to circle the sun.

# Aries

**Motivation and Element:** Cardinal fire

**Symbol:** The ram

**Sun Sign Dates:** March 21 to April 19

**Positive Keywords:** Impulsive, friendly, chatty, active, outgoing, confident, independent, sporty, trusting, optimistic, enthusiastic, energetic

**Negative Keywords:** Bossy, argumentative, challenging, freedom-seeking, naive, unable to compromise

Aries is a fire sign, so they are fast off the mark in everything they do. Their energy levels are doubled up because Aries is also a proactive cardinal sign. "Action without thought" is a good phrase to remember because it explains how Aries expresses that double dose of energy. Their enthusiasm is quickly fired up and as soon as an idea occurs to them, they act on it. Of course, they do think a little bit first, but not for long. That's because their confident optimism assures them everything will work out fine. Aries don't consider the possible pitfalls and failings of a project; they expect things to work out. If it doesn't, no one is more surprised or saddened than our bright, cheerful, and chatty Aries friends.

Aries has unbounded energy and enthusiasm and is filled to the brim with happiness. They have a childlike mindset: "Yesterday didn't exist, tomorrow is too far away, so let's have fun today, right now!" And like children, it is all about the Aries. Things are immediate and personal. Listen to Aries speak and it will be all about their own plans and thoughts. This is how they are meant to be.

The symbol of Aries is the ram. The ram attacks obstacles head-on, and this is how Aries works. Tirelessly optimistic and cheerful, they either ignore obstacles or barge through them, convinced their confidence alone will get them through. Because of this determined optimism they make many mistakes, and it takes Aries a little longer than the other signs to learn from their mistakes.

Because of their straightforward attitude, they are honest, open, and trusting. People often think Aries is naive. And yes, they are. Being so direct and having no artifices or ulterior motives, they do not comprehend underhanded behaviour. What you see is what you get with Aries. They are too busy being busy out in the big, wide world to be interested in manipulating or controlling others—but this also means they are easily misled by unscrupulous people.

What they don't like is people who have a negative attitude, people telling them their ideas won't work, or people who wallow in self-pity and are overly emotional. Aries believe an active body and a busy mind is the panacea to all ailments. They expect others to do as they do; when life knocks them down, they get up and try again. They don't cry, moan, or complain that life isn't fair. They start something new. Consequently, Aries are unsympathetic to others who are less positive, and they're not good at compromising. If you push them too far, expect them to be anything other than they are, or try to control them or curtail their freedom, their worst traits might surface.

Easily frustrated, Aries can be argumentative and confrontational. But, being the sign of springtime, they are like the sunshine and showers of their season, and very soon they are smiling again, all anger forgotten. Aries don't bear grudges and always forgive and forget. Life will knock them down time and again, but up they will rise, just as cheerful, optimistic, and busy as always. It is hard not to like their innocent, warmhearted enthusiasm for every new day.

To recall how Aries work, remember they are cardinal fire and their symbol is the ram and you will be able to figure out how they will act in every circumstance.

# Taurus
## ♉

**Motivation and Element:** Fixed earth

**Symbol:** The bull

**Sun Sign Dates:** April 20 to May 20

**Positive Keywords:** Traditional, stable, reliable, trustworthy, dependable, practical, earthy, family-minded

**Negative Keywords:** Stubborn, determined, opinionated, possessive

Taurus takes its time. Not surprising with a fixed earth sign. Earth is steady and reliable and doesn't like change, and being fixed means the same, so Taurus has a double dose of this unmovable quality. They take their time with everything: jobs, relationships, life itself. Their symbol is the bull for a reason. How does Taurus think and act? Like that. Slowly and cautiously, yet when roused, they are capable of immense strength.

The reason Taureans spend so long deciding something is because they don't like to make mistakes. Mistakes waste time and energy and maybe money as well, all of which are precious commodities to them. Therefore, a great deal of forethought and planning goes into everything they do. Their dreams will all one day come true because Taureans set realistic goals and are prepared to put in sheer hard work over a long period of time to fulfil them. They derive great satisfaction from long-term planning; they don't mind how many years something may take.

Taureans are sensuous. They like the finer things in life. They like food and drink, nice-smelling sheets, and soft carpets under their feet. Comfort is important to them. Knowing this, they typically hold a secure job that will provide them with more than just the essentials. Secure jobs are a rarity these days, but if there is one, they will find it, and they won't sell themselves short. Other people instinctively know a Taurus is someone who can be relied upon and trusted to take on responsibility.

So, once Taurus lands the job, they will look around for a home. That is essential. They need stability and security and their own four walls. Perhaps the house they'd really like hasn't yet been built. That's okay! They will roll up their sleeves and build their own, given the chance; in fact, there is nothing they'd like more.

The next step? Someone to share it all with. A sign ruled by Venus must have a partner. But what sort of partner? Well, that can depend on many factors, but mainly it must be one who will build along with them and not run through all they have worked so hard to achieve. It might be that they saw their ideal partner years before and decided he/she was the one for them. Taureans don't make a move until they have found some security for themselves and have something tangible to offer. Amazingly, their chosen one is often still there, so Taurus goes courting.

That's a very old-fashioned word, but that's Taurus. They are not swayed by the whims of fashion. They go after the partner they want as they do with everything else in life: slowly, systematically, and absolutely determined to succeed. Taurus women lure the partner of their dreams with their earthy charm, their deep and abiding love, and their excellent cooking and caring skills. Taurus men show their loved one how well they can protect and care for them and how financially secure they are.

Ninety-nine percent of the time, Taureans will be successful in love. Occasionally, they aren't. If that happens, Taurus will hold a torch for the rest of their lives. Once their love is given it is almost impossible for them to change tack. Somehow, they get on with their lives. They just take it day by day, putting one foot in front of the other. No drama, no tears, just a sad acceptance and a love that never dies. It is possible that years later they will go in search of their first love and, if the timing is right, finally marry them.

Think of the image of a bull and that Taurus is fixed earth and it will be easy to predict how Taureans will act in any circumstance.

# Gemini
## ♊

**Motivation and Element:** Mutable air

**Symbol:** The twins

**Sun Sign Dates:** May 21 to June 21

**Positive Keywords:** Versatile, quick-witted, great communicator, slick, clever, fun, adaptable

**Negative Keywords:** Fickle, superficial, unreliable, restless, avoids commitment

All the signs have differing motivations. Gemini does everything for mental stimulation because it is an air sign. But it is also mutable, which means flexible and changeable. Because of this, material security, long-lasting relationships, and a secure job are not of any interest to a true Gemini. They are restless people, always seeking new information. They are the messengers of the zodiac, and their job is to drop information as they pass by. A true Gemini will flit through life like a butterfly, collecting and delivering information, and will rarely have an interest in anything lasting. Consequently, they are impossible to pin down and have a reputation for being unreliable. And they are not meant, astrologically speaking, to stay in one place for long.

When it comes to relationships, they are always keen to start one, but as they are not overly physical or sentimental, the initial attraction is usually mental rapport. If there is a good intellectual connection, the physical side will of course follow, but it is never the be-all and end-all for Gemini. They are not really romantic or passionate in the accepted sense.

When Geminis go out, it will be to the latest restaurant or club. Rubbing shoulders with the rich and famous is high on their list of priorities—they need to know what is going on, who is wearing whom, and who is saying what. Staying in and watching TV does not appeal to a Gemini. Even a mature Gemini will want to be out partying and having fun. They believe life is for living at any age, and their need for information and conversation is a powerful force. Words are their forte; that talk-show host or witty and quick-thinking comedian is probably a Gemini. They adore playing with words and have many a caustic (but hilarious) one-liner up their sleeve or, more likely, they'll invent one on the spot.

If a relationship doesn't work out, Geminis won't lose any sleep over it. Life offers so many other exciting possibilities, and they want to try them all. If allowed personal freedom, they will explore life to the fullest, and it has to be said that Geminis are great to be around. Informative, talkative, lighthearted, fun, always willing to go somewhere and do something—it is impossible to resist their friendliness and charm. Attempt to suppress them with rigid rules—or any rules, for that matter—and they will soon slip away.

The symbol for Gemini is the twins, and yes, there are two people in one Gemini, interchangeable twins. One might be lovely while the other is snappy, irritable, and sharply critical. They are only human, after all, and if Geminis feel trapped or bored, the worst side of their nature will surface. Luckily, they have no base motives, so they have no interest at all in hurting others, intentionally or otherwise. A few snappy remarks are about the worst they will do.

You may have heard that every Gemini has two of everything, one for each twin. Most have at least two marriages during their lifetime due to their inability to tolerate the mundane or predictable. Geminis like change and variety, so the more opportunities there are, the happier they will be.

If you remember that Geminis are mutable air and their symbol is the twins, you will be able to predict how they will act in any circumstance.

# Cancer

**Motivation and Element:** Cardinal water

**Symbol:** The crab

**Sun Sign Dates:** June 22 to July 22

**Positive Keywords:** Protective, sensitive, emotional, sentimental, vulnerable, caring

**Negative Keywords:** Smothering, overly emotional, moody, easily hurt

Despite being a cardinal sign, Cancerians are riddled with insecurities. Why? Because this is how water works. It is emotional. It has feelings. Deep feelings. Feelings that go up and down, this way and that, like the ocean—ebbing and flowing, constantly changing. Consequently, mood swings are an intrinsic part of Cancerian nature. So is their ability to console and sympathise with others who are suffering. They are tremendously understanding because they comprehend emotional pain and really do empathise. For water signs, and especially for Cancer, things hurt—every barb, every slight, every rejection. Unkind words go straight to their heart, and they can sit for hours going over and over conversations, wondering why this person said this or did that.

Each water sign reacts in a different way to emotional pain. Cancer retreats inside its shell. Their sign is the crab. Outwardly, you may see no change, but inwardly they are grieving. That is when they go in search of comfort in the form of old photographs—and yes, it will probably be those old albums with faded photographs of long-gone family members. The past has a rosy glow, because people were nicer then, weren't they? More polite, more refined, more decent? That is what they would like to think, anyway. Being sentimental, they love those sepia photographs and can study faces for ages, wondering what they were thinking. Were they happy? Consequently, Cancerians never throw anything away. When they are feeling hurt by someone's word or deed, they retreat back to the past, shed a tear, wallow for a while in their ocean of emotions, and condemn the world as a hard, unfeeling place. But after a while they dry their tears and get back to real life because they are, after all, a cardinal sign.

When it comes to forgiveness, a Cancer can forgive anything but a personal betrayal because it completely undermines their fragile self-esteem. That's why they spend their lives building a world where they are protected and surrounded by their own loving family. Their main aim and purpose in life is to create emotional security.

Cancerians take it hard when they lose anything they consider to be theirs. When they choose a partner, it is for life. They need to know someone is there for them when the world knocks them down, someone they can trust and rely on. In return they offer deep devotion and are capable of great personal sacrifice for those they love.

Cancer has its negative points, too, as do all the signs. This overriding need for emotional security is so great they do their best to provide it for others, and often their children will bear the brunt of this overprotective attitude. Problems come when the children want to fly the nest because Cancerians take it harder than most to adjust to no longer being needed. Also, because of their sensitive emotional nature, they often take umbrage at slights no one else would notice. This can make others feel they are having to walk on eggshells in an effort to avoid hurting Cancer, whom they may perceive as overly emotional, overly protective, and too needy.

To remember how Cancer acts, just recollect that they are a cardinal water sign and their symbol is the crab.

# Leo
♌

**Motivation and Element:** Fixed fire

**Symbol:** The lion

**Sun Sign Dates:** July 23 to August 22

**Positive Keywords:** Warm, loyal, commanding, confident, generous, able

**Negative Keywords:** Stubborn, opinionated, conceited, needs constant praise

Need someone to organise an event? Find a Leo. Being a fire sign, they are full of energy and drive. Not only that, but they are fantastic organisers and planners and know just the right people to approach to get things done. You won't see them rolling up their own sleeves, but they have a way of effortlessly getting others to do their bidding. Maybe it's their renowned charm and that glow in their eyes that other people simply cannot resist! They do not boss, they command, and all others can do is obey.

These are the people in charge of troops on the front line, the heads of charitable organisations, the ones directing those who fight forest fires, or the person organising everyone when there has been a road accident. In whatever life-and-death situation they are called on to face, Leos calmly and capably sort everything out. They have courage and confidence, and people listen and follow their instructions. What, then, is a word of praise in such circumstances?

Praise? Yes, praise. It's their be-all and end-all, the motivation behind all their efforts. Despite all that confident charm, Leos cannot function at their best unless they are admired, respected, and deferred to. They have a natural dignity that just can't accept failure or criticism. Criticism, particularly, affects them deeply, but they are too proud to show they care. Leos really do need to be number one and to have that lofty position recognised by their adoring public. To that end, Leos will literally exhaust themselves trying to succeed.

Honest praise brings out the very best in them, and the very best of Leo is wonderful. Leos are ruled by the sun itself and glow with animal magnetism and personal charisma. Leo is the sign of royalty. Its symbol is the lion, the king of the jungle. Have you ever seen royalty doing the mundane tasks? Being ruled by the sun, they exude warmth, love, affection, and loyalty, given the right atmosphere. A word of praise is all they ask, and in return you can bask in their exciting good humour, joy, utter loyalty, and willingness to sacrifice everything for those who adore them. Leos give a great deal in return for a simple thank you.

Negatives? Being a fixed sign means Leos can be stubborn and opinionated. Sometimes their commanding manner may just feel bossy. They are especially bossy with their family. Leos will endeavour to organise things in a way that shows themselves off because a Leo's life is all about showiness. They are an actor, and the world is their stage. Consequently, they are always aware of how they look and present themselves, and this extends to their family. This can get tiring for loved ones. Equally annoying is their need for constant praise. For a commanding, loyal, and fearless sign, they are remarkably insecure. But if you give them too much praise, they can get conceited! It is a fine line but when the balance is found, no one will protect, love, and shelter their family more than a Leo.

Because Leo is a fixed sign, they are also stubborn. Their innate pride makes it impossible for them to apologise or admit they were in the wrong. It will always be up to others to smooth the waters, but Leo accepts their forgiveness immediately. Fire signs do not hold grudges and they enjoy being happy and carefree, which is why they dislike negative, emotional, grudge-holding people and avoid them as much as they can.

Think of Leos as not only the lion, but as fixed fire, and you can easily figure out how they will act in all circumstances.

# Virgo
## ♍

**Motivation and Element:** Mutable earth

**Symbol:** The earth maiden

**Sun Sign Dates:** August 23 to September 22

**Positive Keywords:** Practical, service-minded, dutiful, self-denying, observant, detail-driven

**Negative Keywords:** Nitpicky, fussy, critical, worrier

Virgo is an earth sign. They are grounded and dutiful. Their symbol is the earth maiden, who attends to practical details, so Virgo notices everything. Nothing bypasses their laser vision. While you are speaking, they will watch you carefully, listen to your words, and observe your movements. They will notice your accent, your clothes, and if your nails and shoes are clean, and they will suss any hidden motives you have.

If a Virgo visits you at home, they will be able to describe the colour of your carpet and the design of your curtains, plus what crockery you use and if your bathroom is clean. A bit scary, huh? Imagine how they feel, then, seeing all these details with such clarity, yet knowing they simply don't have the time or energy to get everything neat and tidy and organised the way they'd like.

It is easy for Virgos to get bogged down in minor details and lose the overall picture. That is when they need the advice of a less analytical person, someone who can lift them out of the doldrums. Yes, they can get very low in spirits at times. There is so much around them that needs doing. Virgos have a never-ending, monumental to-do list, and they fear that they will never achieve the goals they have set for themselves.

Virgos are reliable caregivers. If they have a family, the needs of their loved ones will always come first, even if that involves personal sacrifice. They are good at being selfless and do it often. Virgos sometimes feel as if they don't even exist because they spend most of their lives doing things for other people, cleaning up messes—both literally and figuratively.

On the surface, Virgos always present as cool, calm, and unruffled. Their clothes will be immaculate even if you arrive at their door unexpectedly at seven in the morning; these are the people that manage to look neat and tidy even if they've just run a marathon. Most Virgos have large, clear eyes, but their well-groomed appearance is another giveaway of their astrological sign. If you still aren't sure, wait for a moment and a Virgo will absently pick a bit of fluff off your jacket or clean the table with their hand while waiting for the meeting to start. In a restaurant, they are the ones tidying up the menus or the sauce bottles and condiments. They will comment on the cleanliness of the place, the speed of the service, and the cost of the meal. You are allowed, at this point, to smile to yourself—Virgo spotted.

The negative side of Virgo is their overly critical tongue. It is impossible for them not to verbalise the faults and failings of others, which they see so clearly. Because the mundane jobs are never-ending, there is always work for Virgo, so naturally they start nitpicking. Their exercise and eating regime is honed to a fine art, and Virgos wonder why others can't look after themselves the way they do, why others can't seem to manage to stay fit and neat and tidy, and why others can't clean up after themselves. So yes, they will moan about the mess you leave and nag you to get fit and eat a better diet. Virgos are always worrying about all the jobs they have to on their to-do list (and they are always adding more!), so they think if others were tidier, life would be easier. It must be hard to see work everywhere, yet Virgo does its best. They are kind to everyone and serve dutifully and faithfully, but—it has to be said—not always uncomplainingly!

The icing on the cake, though, is a Virgo's sexiness. You think I'm joking? You might be thinking, *They look so cool and calm and in control. How can they let go and be sexy?* Well, just drag a Virgo away from work, dim the lights (so they can't see more jobs to add to their list), play some gentle music, pour them a drink, and their famous passion will emerge. Underneath that dutiful exterior lurks a deeply passionate and earthy sex god/goddess just waiting to be awakened.

To work out how Virgos will act in any circumstance, just remember they are mutable earth and their symbol is the earth maiden, who attends to practical details.

# Libra

**Modality and Element:** Cardinal air

**Symbol:** The scales

**Sun Sign Dates:** September 23 to October 23

**Positive Keywords:** Harmonious, balance, fair, equal, compromising, logical

**Negative Keywords:** Lazy, snobbish, can use people, unemotional

Libra is an air sign. Air uses its brain. The physical is fine, the emotional ... well, they'd rather not go down that route in any way, shape, or form. But when it comes to thinking, discussions, and analytical arguments—and let's use the word *arguments* loosely, as Libras rarely argue; they make their point with clear fairness—they are suddenly all ears and attention.

There is nothing Libras like more than discussing something. Doing something is quite another matter. Thinking takes all their energy, which isn't inexhaustible at the best of times. By the time they have fully weighed all the pros and cons of a particular plan and made a logical decision, they need to go have a rest.

Libras are nothing if not fair. Their sign is the scales for a reason. They spend their lives trying to make reasoned, sound judgments, weighing all arguments on their scales to make sure their decisions are balanced. They are quite capable of putting themselves in someone else's shoes and coming up with a logical decision, but shouting, anger, and any form of aggression upsets their delicate balancing act. They need peace and quiet and soothing music to think.

Pluses? They are lovely to look at, both male and female. Libras are ruled by Venus, so of course they are beautiful. When their scales are in balance, they are the most gentle, attractive, well-dressed, peaceful people you could hope to meet. Even in old clothes, they manage to look stylish and clean. Even with their hair tousled, they look gorgeous. Bad hair days are not something Libras ever suffer from, not that you'd notice anyway. Their smile could melt ice.

When the scales have dipped, you will find Libras on the sofa, silent and exhausted. Never mind that the grass needs mowing, the ironing is piling up, or the dust is an inch thick, they will be unable to motivate themselves. But even when Libras feel grumpy and lazy, they are still polite and courteous and kind and lovely. They won't take it out on you as long as you leave them alone until they get their scales in balance again. They don't like being out of balance any more than you do.

A useful piece of information: Don't ever ask a Libra for an opinion on what you are wearing or to choose an outfit for you. They clearly see every side of that question and in an effort to be kind, they will describe how each item suits you—and how each doesn't. It takes a strong ego to survive that gentle but thorough dissemination of your good and bad features. The thing is, they are right, and you know they are right, but being told the facts so clearly and logically is somehow crushing, no matter how kindly expressed.

One thing Libras can't abide is uncleanliness in their home, office, or partner. It upsets their fragile balance. Their surroundings need to be peaceful and preferably luxurious, though they'll settle for very nice if finances dictate luxury is not possible, and their partner better shape up or ship out. They don't like unpleasantness thrust under their noses; they don't mind talking about it, but they don't want to face it. Their cardinal energy goes into thinking and making decisions, not cleaning up other people's messes—or even their own, come to that. Not that they will create much, being so neat and tidy. They can ignore a to-do list when their scales are out of balance, but would love it even more if their partner did the dirty work and left them to rest and think.

Because they are a cardinal sign, they are proactive in achieving the above-average lifestyle they need to remove themselves from the rougher, scarier elements of life. To keep themselves in balance, Libras need luxury and are perfectly able to use their considerable intellect to work for what they want. However, if a rich partner appears in view, all their antennae will be alerted, and Libras will leave no stone unturned to add to their stockpile of luxuries by marrying for money.

A Libra's worst faults are laziness and their dislike of getting their hands dirty, but with their considerable charm they always manage to rope in others to help with tasks they feel are demeaning. Libras easily manipulate people with their disarming charm.

To remember how Libras work, think of their symbol, the scales, and that they are cardinal air.

# Scorpio
## ♏

**Motivation and Element:** Fixed water

**Symbol:** The scorpion

**Sun Sign Dates:** October 24 to November 21

**Positive Keywords:** Passionate, intense, deeply emotional, loyal, driven

**Negative Keywords:** Stubborn, opinionated, secretive, vengeful, jealous

How can you spot a Scorpio? Look for the one who is cool, calm, and apparently uninterested. That disinterest is a front.

It is unusual for a water sign to hide their feelings; often it is easy to spot one because they react with tears, sympathy, and compassion. Not Scorpio. They prefer to hide their sensitivity and vulnerability behind a facade of implacability.

The watchwords with Scorpio are control and passion. Let's start with the first. Not only do they control themselves, thus hiding their emotions, they will also try to control their partner. This is not a Taurus possessiveness. This is far more than wanting to possess. Scorpios want to metaphorically strip you bare and see into your very soul, to know exactly where you are coming from and what you want from life and from them. They are naturally suspicious of people. Surely there is an agenda or a hidden motive? They always have both, so they cannot understand people who do not or those who appear too good to be true. Can anyone be *that* good? They doubt it.

When Scorpios have stripped you of all your reserves—mentally, physically, and emotionally—and they find you okay to trust, they will accept you as a lover or partner. But they will always be watching and waiting. Their control over you is their knowledge of your inner workings; now they know how to manipulate you, cleverly using subtle means to achieve their ends. So clever are they, most people have no idea Scorpio is pulling the strings.

Now we come to passion. You think it is only sexual? Not in the least. Scorpios feel passionate about everything and anything. No matter what they choose to do, they will investigate, explore, and research; they want to know all the angles and possible pitfalls, all the positives and negatives so they aren't caught off-guard.

If a Scorpio has an idea, you won't hear it until it has been thoroughly examined from every angle. Only then will they run it past you to see your reaction. Yes, reaction. Your opinion is not required. If they have decided on something, why would they need you to second it? They trust no one's instincts but their own. They think. They decide. And they are a fixed sign, so they are stubborn and opinionated.

Scorpios feel passionately about everything, and yes, that does include sex. A new person in their life has to be understood, and sex is a very good way of seeing people with all their defences down. It's unlikely theirs will be, though, even at the height of passion. They keep one eye open at all times. You are simply the next thing they are investigating, and they want to understand everything about you. To that end, Scorpios are not attracted to flimsy lightweights, but to those who have the capacity to love them back. People who intrigue Scorpios last a lot longer than an open book, so give them a challenge. Make it harder for them to get to know you. Play it cool and say no now and then; they love nothing more than an enigma.

Now that we have dealt with the control and passion issues, let's discuss the base aspects: jealousy and suspicion. When feelings run deep, this is what happens. And, being naturally suspicious, when Scorpios have committed themselves to someone, they are tormented by these two passions.

So how can you beat Scorpio at their own game? The simple answer is, you can't. They are masters at the arts of secrecy and investigation. But let's give you a head start: Their Achilles' heel is their need for emotional security. Going through life alone is not possible for a Scorpio. They have so much to give and such deep love that it has to have a focus. They too want to relax sometimes and trust. It must be hard being forever on guard.

Whatever Scorpios do in life, they do for keeps. If you are in their life, in some capacity you have passed the first hurdle. You've been allowed in. So just keep going and you might find the highest accolade of all: complete acceptance. If you are loved by a Scorpio, you are truly loved. There is nothing wishy-washy about their complete devotion, overwhelming passion, and utter loyalty. They will fight to the death for their partner and children.

Just don't forget that underneath, they are waiting to pounce. Never give them a reason to. Their symbol is the scorpion, so if you cross a Scorpio, beware the sting in its tail. They always take revenge, even though they may bide their time in doing so. From a caustic word to outright revenge, it will come sooner or later, so be warned!

This intensity comes from being a fixed water sign. Water is emotion, but fix it in one place and it becomes a deep, black ocean of unfathomable depth. The deeper you dive in, the darker it appears; emotions are condensed and heightened. This is Scorpio.

To predict how they might act, remember that Scorpios are a fixed water sign and their symbol is the scorpion.

# Sagittarius

**Motivation and Element:** Mutable fire

**Symbol:** The archer

**Sun Sign Dates:** November 22 to December 21

**Positive Keywords:** Searching, learning, philosophising, travel, foreign places

**Negative Keywords:** Unreliable, restless, unpredictable, craves personal freedom

Sagittarius is a fire sign and its symbol is the archer, firing his arrows into the air one after another. Think of those arrows as ideas. This is how Sagittarians work, with many irons in the fire and numerous projects on the go. Hardly have they finished one before they are off on another adventure, following another idea, or studying something different. They can keep half a dozen things on the go at once and easily juggle them all; that's how they like it, because then boredom will never set in. They move effortlessly from one thing to another. Sometimes they finish things, sometimes they don't.

Usually, Sagittarians are so busy being busy—traveling, talking, seeking, learning, and exploring—they don't stay around long enough to see what impact they have made on people's lives, nor do they really care. For them, it is all about experiences and adventures (lots of them!), all of which teach them something, all of which add to their personal philosophy.

It is very easy for a Sagittarius to lose track of themselves. They are fire signs, after all, and as such, they are active and impulsive. They never say no to invitations because they might miss something. Being mutable, they are also a fan of variety and movement. Sagittarians like to be free to wander, explore, meet new people, and see new things.

How do you spot one? It is the person who is warm, cheerful, and friendly who always has an open door. They have a huge group of friends from all walks of life, and they prefer to have a busy schedule. An empty day is anathema to them. Heaven is a place to be at any given hour, preferably all different.

Sagittarians are renowned for their honesty. In a world of fake praise, it's refreshing to know someone speaks the truth. But honesty can hurt. Sometimes we don't want the blunt truth that we are looking awful. So, rule number one: Do not ask a Sagittarius for their opinion unless you can take it straight and unvarnished. They are truthful to the point of rudeness and are renowned for speaking their minds and saying the most outrageous things!

Like all mutable signs, they are quite capable of starting out down one path and switching direction halfway through. And, also like all mutable signs, they resist being tied down. They might eventually settle for family life and a mortgage, but they will never feel really bound by it. A sensible partner will give a Sagittarius room to roam, but perhaps a large house and garden would do, a place with a spacious study and at least one wall full of travel books or enlightening subjects. If they can't travel in reality, Sagittarians can happily travel in their minds. Give them the illusion of freedom and they might stay around forever—but don't put any money on it.

Sagittarians love people. Consequently, be prepared to have a house full of friends on short notice and to host lavish parties—probably more lavish than they can really afford. They adore entertaining on a grand scale. If you are looking for stability, a sizeable bank account balance, and routine, this is not the sign to fall for. On the other hand, if you think a full, happy, and exciting life is your thing, hitch your star to the heart of a Sagittarius and hold on tight. It might be a bumpy ride, but it will be oh so much fun.

The negatives are obvious: unreliability, unpredictable behaviour, and the propensity to let people down because something more interesting turned up. Obviously, Sagittarians are fun people to be around, but because they resist any form of commitment or restriction, it's best to enjoy their company when they appear and to accept that you never know when you will see them again.

To remember how Sagittarius acts, think of their symbol, the archer, and that they are a mutable fire sign.

# Capricorn
♑

**Motivation and Element:** Cardinal earth

**Symbol:** The goat

**Sun Sign Dates:** December 22 to January 19

**Positive Keywords:** Traditional, persevering, ambitious, patient, family-focused

**Negative Keywords:** Status-seeking, snobbish, dull, melancholy

Earth signs are reliable. They are trustworthy. They have staying power. This is because all earth signs, but Capricorn in particular, want to build something lasting, something that will outlive them. It could be a family line, but they would prefer it to be something in bricks and mortar—or in bank bonds or gold bars!

Yet, earth signs are not mercenary. Not really. It isn't about the money, it's about the durability of their life and all of their efforts—and their efforts will be considerable. Earth signs don't like change as a rule, but Capricorn is a cardinal sign, which means they will not hesitate to move on if it is necessary. Capricorns will move houses, move jobs, move countries even! They are proactive when it comes to their status. They seek the highest job, the best position, the most prestigious house. Any and all accolades are most welcome, but not unless accompanied by something solid in the way of remuneration, because money means stability and security. It means something to leave to the generations who come after.

Despite all setbacks and difficulties, Capricorns carry on, trudging their way through any and all obstacles. This is because their symbol is the goat, who surefootedly weaves its way to the top pinnacle. That is their life's aim.

When they get there, when they finally reach that top position, they are inclined to be a bit snobbish about those on the lower rungs of life's ladder; they prefer to mix with their social equals.

They approach relationships with the same steady, sensible head. What would be the point of choosing a partner who doesn't understand the need for security, who will waste all they have worked so hard for? They seek someone traditional, worthy, and reliable, a person who won't ever let them down in any way—financially, morally, or ethically. There is nothing a Capricorn would hate more than an embarrassing partner, so they make very sure they pick carefully.

All this hard work takes its toll on their moods, and this is the sign renowned for depression. Not having a lightness of mind and heart, they can easily get bogged down in duty and responsibility. They find it hard to lighten up and almost impossible to party. They aren't social animals, and they don't have the social graces to be. They are certainly polite, but rarely are they glib.

To remember how Capricorns will act in any circumstance, think of them being a cardinal earth sign and having the goat as their symbol.

# Aquarius
≋

**Motivation and Element:** Fixed air

**Symbol:** The water carrier

**Sun Sign Dates:** January 20 to February 18

**Positive Keywords:** Individual, independent, original, calm

**Negative Keywords:** Stubborn, unpredictable, determined to maintain their independence and personal freedom

Aquarians are unique individuals. So unique it is almost impossible to pin down what they will be like because they will all be different, not only from everyone else but from every other Aquarian. Their symbol is the water carrier, but the glyph is two jagged lines. The water they carry is their humanitarian drive, and the jagged lines express their eccentric and unique brain patterns.

Let's assume you have an Aquarian standing in front of you. What will they be like? To start with, they are an air sign, so they are detached and logical. Like all air signs, they don't like or understand emotional behaviour and prefer to avoid it.

They have a need to be different. Usually, they express this in their attire. They are likely to turn up at a wedding in jeans and a T-shirt and to wear their suit down to the bar. If you say wear black, they will wear white. It's important to them to express their uniqueness. Still, they turned up for the event, and that is something. The sudden urge to display their personal freedom didn't overtake them. That is always a possibility with an Aquarius. Just when you are up to your ears in something and need some support, they are likely to simply walk out. Naturally, this drives people mad, but an Aquarius won't care. They are who they are; that's the fixity of their sign. They won't change, not for anyone, not even you. Don't like it? Then go. But they won't chase you, so make sure you mean it before you pack your bags.

Fixed air is a difficult concept to grasp. The element of air means Aquarians are cool and logical and unmoved by appeals to their compassion. The fixed bit means they don't care what others think. They are who they are, and they don't give a hoot what you say. All fixed signs are stubborn, just in different ways. Their fixity is in the fact they are not going to change who they are.

Aquarians do feel, of course, but in a detached, observant sort of way. Or rather, they don't so much feel as analyse why other people are upset. They view life from an emotional distance and rarely get personally involved, even if it is their own partner or children. They don't stop to wonder if anyone needs anything from them because they do not take to the role of carer very well. Their minds are always off somewhere else. They are probably inventing something or solving some obscure problem. If Aquarians see someone who needs help, it sort of registers somewhere, but then it passes them by as they wander through life analysing and questioning.

It's important to remember that they are not intentionally unkind. There is nothing vindictive or mean about them. Nothing is personal to an Aquarian. It's simply that they are elsewhere. Ask where, and they will shrug. *They* don't even know.

If an Aquarius gets married and settles down—and most of them do—it is usually just an experiment. They want to see what it is like and what everyone is making a fuss about. They want to understand why others seem to need security so much, even though this is something alien to their natures. Try as they might to relate in a loving way, they find themselves watching, listening, and picking up odd signals. Aquarians are generally faithful in the accepted sense. Human passions such as jealousy, anger, hate, and love are all just curiosities to them. Hem them in and they will find a way to be free. Give them space to be their unique selves and they might hang around.

The negatives are pretty obvious: unpredictable behaviour, unreliability, the need to walk out when life gets tough. Yet, they are calm, friendly, and fun, and they gather friends from all walks of life. Aquarians always have an open door and you can help yourself to anything they have. Security and possessions mean nothing, so they will gladly share what they have. But given their casual attitude to money, it might not be much!

To predict how Aquarians might act, remember they are fixed air and their glyph is the jagged lines of their eccentric brain patterns.

# Pisces

**Motivation and Element:** Mutable water

**Symbol:** The fish

**Sun Sign Dates:** February 19 to March 20

**Positive Keywords:** Sensitive, compassionate, understanding, intuitive

**Negative Keywords:** Unreliable, cool, easily overwhelmed

Pisceans are gentle, sweet, compassionate dreamers who find the stresses of life a bit overwhelming. Being a water sign, everything they do is based on how they feel about something or someone; their decisions have no foundations in logic, which is alien to them, yet they are invariably correct. Pisces is not only water (and therefore intuitive and sensitive), but mutable water: flowing water, forever moving, sometimes in tidal waves, sometimes as a fast-flowing stream, sometimes as a gentle trickle or a sleepy ocean.

There is no way of holding on to a Pisces or of pinning them down. Try to scoop up water and what happens? Whether they are reacting to stress with irritability or swiftly floating downstream to avoid trouble or confrontation, you can be assured they won't hang around if things get difficult.

Pisceans won't argue if they disagree with you; raised voices disturb them. Rather than cause a scene, they will agree with you and then slip away to calmer, less stressful waters. In extreme cases, if a Pisces can't escape physically, they will take to alcohol or drugs. They look for the easiest way out and always take the line of least resistance.

The symbol of Pisces is two fish swimming in opposite directions. Imagine each fish is an idea. Pisces has the ability to understand both of those opposing ideas, and to accept that they are equally fine, which is why they have difficulty deciding on anything. In the end, they invariably do nothing. If they wait, maybe their intuition will give them a clue. Or maybe not. This is how a Pisces exists all of the time—in a dreamy underwater world where signposts are not visible.

Other people are forever taking advantage of them because Pisceans find it hard to say no. Their tender hearts are suckers for a sob story. They have vulnerable hearts but they are intuitive, if not outright clairvoyant, so they generally know when someone is taking advantage of them. Despite that, they will do all they can for anyone in need, then retreat when their job is done.

Oddly, while they are deeply compassionate, there is something slightly detached about them. Their compassion is not passion. Passion is excitable and dramatic, and Pisces is a cool sign. So they are, in fact, quite capable of holding something of themselves back. They know their limits.

Pisceans aren't really of this world. They have one foot in the next, which is why so many of them take the pain that is dumped on them and turn it into works of art. They paint, play music, or act. They understand the deeper meaning of life, but don't ask them to explain it. They won't have the words, just the feelings.

Their most obvious failing is their unreliability. They give their all, but their all is limited. They get easily overwhelmed and stressed. The world, and the way people live life now, is not in harmony with their vibration. They will offer all the sympathy in the world, but when it comes to practical help, they can hardly manage their own lives, let alone take on others' burdens. It's easy for them to listen, sympathise, and express concern. Any more is beyond them.

To understand how Pisceans will react in any circumstances, remember they are mutable water and their symbol is the fish.

## Two
# THE PERSONAL PLANETS

*A*lthough the sky is full of stars and planets, astrology only uses the ten planets closest to us, those that orbit the sun. Their size gives these ten planets a gravitational field of their own, and it is this emanating energy and its effect on us here on Earth that astrologers interpret. The moon is the best example of a close planet that has an influence on us because of its ability to affect Earth's tides and people's moods. Each of the ten planets has an impact on your personality, but in a different way.

The first seven planets—sun, moon, Mercury, Venus, Mars, Jupiter, and Saturn—are called *personal planets* because their energies are strong and we use them in our daily life. The other three planets—Uranus, Neptune, and Pluto—are so far away and take so long to progress through each astrological sign that they are called *outer planets*. We will learn all about them in a later chapter. In this chapter, we will focus on the first six of the personal planets. The seventh, Saturn, has a chapter all to itself. This is because Saturn is synonymous with karmic lessons, so it needs a more thorough investigation.

# Sun

**Affects:** Will, energy, enthusiasm, sense of identity

The sun is the most important planet, and in chapter 1 we looked at how your sun sign is used to express your true self. The other six personal planets are dotted around your chart at your moment of birth. Every planet moves at different speeds, which is why specific dates cannot be assigned to them. The astrological sign all these planets were in when you were born gives a unique insight into how you will react and behave in certain circumstances. Using this deeper knowledge, you can become more than a mere astrological observer—you become a predictor of behaviour patterns.

# Moon
☾

**Affects:** Emotional responses, feelings, sensitivities, the child within, how you respond emotionally

The second most important planet in your birth chart is the moon. It rules Cancer.

The moon is all about emotion. In your birth chart, the astrological sign of your moon placement shows how you express emotions, what you seek at an emotional level, and what nurtures and comforts you. Your moon sign also has a role to play in love. Because it's important to be able to emotionally relate to your chosen partner, your moon signs need to compatible. In general, but particularly in close relationships, we tend to better relate to people who have their sun in the same astrological sign as our moon, or to those who have their moon in the same element as ours—fire, earth, air, or water. If this is the case, you tend to understand each other's needs better.

Pull up your birth chart and find which astrological sign your moon is in. Using what you already know about the elements (fire, earth, air, and water) and motivations (cardinal, fixed, and mutable), see if you can interpret your moon sign. Then check out the following interpretations to see how well you did.

## *Moon in Aries (Cardinal Fire)*

This is not a happy pairing. Planets in Aries act assertively and fast. Maybe not quite the way one should approach love!

In the cardinal fire of Aries, the moon cannot express its tender side. It becomes unfeeling and lacking in empathy. Aries is a warm, kindhearted sign, but it is also tough and no-nonsense. This gives Aries the ability to quickly move on to another partner if a relationship isn't working out. Being easily bored, desirous of personal freedom, and keen on emotional excitement does not bode well for long-term relationships unless their partner is incredibly tolerant.

They may not be a romantic sign, but Aries moon people are fun and exciting. Generous too, as well as honest, trusting, and straightforward. If they say they like you, believe them. They don't play games.

Like everything else they do, falling in love is, for them, a quick affair. If they see someone they like, they head straight over and ask them out. They really can't be bothered with nuances. Tenderness is alien to an Aries moon, so yes, they lack the subtleties of romantic foreplay. But if you like people who are direct, then an Aries moon could be the perfect match for you!

Being so optimistic and confident, Aries moons expect relationships to work and always avoid the obvious warning signs. When a partner is annoyed with them, they either won't notice or won't even care. They don't hold themselves responsible for someone else's happiness; Aries moons expect others to get on with it and sort themselves out because that's what they do.

Aries moons don't want to tie themselves to someone who is too emotional, too needy, or too reliant. They want their partner to be as independent as they are. Emotionally, they are not supportive or sympathetic. They will listen to their partner's problems and then offer a positive way out of their difficulties, but they have no time for or interest in long, drawn-out drama.

The positives of an Aries moon are their warm, affectionate nature and their trusting belief in their partners. Give them room to be independent and don't lean on them emotionally, and a partnership with an Aries moon can work just fine.

### *Moon in Taurus (Fixed Earth)*

The moon, by definition, is emotional. In the fixity of Taurus, the fluctuations of emotion are dampened down, which makes for a steady and reliable emotional life. It also gives Taurus the ability to tolerate situations others would deem impossible simply to avoid an upheaval; any planet situated in Taurus resists change. Taurus moons handle difficult situations by doing nothing, instead allowing time to pass.

All fixed signs like things being done their own way. They are stubborn. This applies to Taurus in particular because the earth element is combined with fixity. This is a challenge for anyone whose partner has a Taurus moon. Once Taurus moons have decided on something, that's it. Creating a dramatic scene will not budge them one bit. To be fair, Taurus moons will listen. They will stand and take their partner's torrent of complaints and even hysterical anger. It will be water off a duck's back, though. Watching someone have an emotional breakdown is, for a Taurus moon, like observing someone from an alien planet. They simply do not understand it.

However, this fixity means Taurus moons make excellent long-term partners. Once committed, they stay around. No wild interludes for them. They enjoy all the sensual pleasures of life, and if they can get them within the security and safety of their current relationship, they will look no further.

Taurus is a sensuous earth sign. Taurus moons like luxury, but they won't waste money. Ideally, their partner will be as sensible, grounded, and financially astute as them because they will not tolerate someone spending unwisely. They enjoy a nice meal, a good glass of wine, and all of the other tangible pleasures of life, and that includes sex. It's easy to catch a Taurus moon by offering all of the above—but Taurus loves forever, so be warned. Play the long game because Taurus will be hard to shake off!

### *Moon in Gemini (Mutable Air)*

Air signs are unemotional. Mutable air is cool, detached, and hard to pin down. Because of this, emotional dramas frighten Gemini moons, especially if they foresee it might involve them in some sort of commitment of their time and/or emotion. They like to move through life lightly, so emotions are apt to be cloying and restricting. Gemini moons disappear immediately if anyone endeavours to manipulate them into a commitment.

Gemini moons aren't overly physical, so while they are as interested in sex as the rest of the human race, they are not wildly passionate. They fall in love with a person's mind first. Conversation and shared ideas are the most important aspects in both friendships and relationships.

Another stumbling block? Gemini moons don't like to be around people who are ill, physically or mentally. It is not they don't care; they simply don't have the tools to deal with it. They prefer partners who deal with their own emotional stuff.

Okay, that is the negatives over with. What about the positives? Well, Gemini moons are exciting and interesting. They are always up for trying something new. They are not lazy, boring, or overly materialistic. Wherever they lay their hat is home. They won't make emotional demands, nor will they use manipulation to get their way. If their partner doesn't want to do something, they won't mind, but they may find someone else who does.

Long-term commitment is difficult for Gemini moons. Mutable air does not really need security and stability—it needs stimulation. It is questionable how much stimulation the nitty-gritty of life can provide, which is why most Gemini moons end up having more than one marriage.

### Moon in Cancer (Cardinal Water)

This is the perfect pairing. The moon rules the sign of Cancer, and this moon placement can express Cancer's deeply emotional nature.

Water signs are all compassionate and intuitive, but Cancer is especially sensitive. It takes a long time and a lot of trust for Cancer to come out of its shell and commit to someone. Cancer's symbol is the crab, remember? They wear their shell to protect their vulnerability. Usually, Cancer moons are naturally aware of who will hurt them and who won't, but they are not infallible. If they find their trust has been misplaced, they are inconsolable. They never really recover from the loss of someone they loved, and each new hurt opens up those old wounds. Cancer moons tend to wallow in their emotions.

Thankfully, they are a cardinal sign. After a while they will dry their eyes, climb back in their shell, and go out into the world because of their overriding need to create emotional and financial security for themselves and their loved ones.

Because Cancer moons empathise with everyone in physical, mental, or emotional pain, the line is often blurred between their own pain and the suffering of others. It can make them overprotective and overly emotional, so much so that friends, family, and partners often feel they are walking on eggshells in an attempt not to upset Cancer moons. It must be hard being ruled by such an emotional planet, but understanding when to draw the line is a must for their own emotional well-being.

Cancer moons love deeply and need a partner who will understand their requirement for emotional shelter when the world has been unkind, a partner who can wrap their arms around them and reassure them they are loved. In return, they offer a kind of wholehearted devotion rarely found.

### Moon in Leo (Fixed Fire)

Being a fire sign, Leo moons are warm and affectionate. Their symbol, the lion, reflects their need to love and be loved, to look after their family, and to have that family respect, admire, and appreciate them.

Leo moons have a wonderfully youthful, almost childlike, love of life and an innocent belief in joy for its own sake. Leo moons love to dress up, party, and have fun. They like the circus, funfairs, theatres, festivals, and any opportunity to enjoy life to the fullest. Leo moons also adore being in love and are at their happiest when their loved one gazes at them adoringly and waxes on about how wonderful they are!

But the fixed nature of Leo mixed with the emotional water element of the moon means they can get angry quickly. They may posture and pace and get bossy, but underneath they are not really lions—they are pussycats. Perhaps the Leo moon is upset that they did a lot for someone and weren't given the right amount of appreciation or praise in return. It's easy to stop their roaring. Reassure them that they are number one and keep on reassuring them, always and forever. If you stroke a Leo moon, they will purr. But if you ignore their efforts, they will roar or stalk off to seek someone who actually does appreciate all they do.

A Leo moon will never apologise. They are fixed, which equals stubborn. Being both stubborn and proud makes it impossible for them to back down, even if they know they are in the wrong. However, fire signs are always magnanimous. They forgive immediately if someone else makes the first move.

As long as Leo moons are admired, they are self-sacrificing in the extreme. Their loyalty is a given, but like all fire signs, they do want a bit of excitement along the way. They are not naturally flighty, but they might resort to a fling if they feel unappreciated by their nearest and dearest, so whether they stay put or stray is entirely up to you.

### *Moon in Virgo (Mutable Earth)*

Put the moon in this sign and it creates someone who gets easily irritated by things most of us don't even notice: someone munching an apple too loudly, a lopsided picture on a wall, a repetitive squeak from a car, or a tea-stained table. A Virgo moon's mood is affected when things are out of place, untidy, or downright chaotic. Details are the focus and the bane of their existence.

Virgo moons are modest and unassuming, and they find it hard to believe that they are lovable. They are plagued by inner doubts as to their worthiness. How can anyone love them when they see their own faults and failings so glaringly?

This makes them emotionally shy and reserved—at first. If a Virgo moon feels loved and secure in their relationship, they are passionate people. They are an earth sign, after all, and are earthy in their needs. Virgos are very reserved until they feel secure, but once they do, there is nothing inhibited about them, especially not in the bedroom!

Virgo is the sign of service, so Virgo moons do a lot for their partner—sometimes too much. They find it almost impossible to say no. Being mutable, they are actually quite flexible.

Once a relationship is over and they have licked their wounds for a while, Virgo moons will seek out someone else because they do need a partner. All those carefully reserved emotions are just a cover for their deep insecurities. They may be a touch more reserved with their next partner, though, and take longer to thaw out. They are always cautious when approaching a relationship, and repeated failures will only make them more so.

## *Moon in Libra (Cardinal Air)*

The moon is not comfortable in air signs. Air signs are happy to discuss emotion but would far rather ignore the gushing sentiments associated with emotional matters. When their partner starts showing emotional tendencies, they feel alarmed.

Yet, Libras need a partner. They are lost without someone else, even if it's only a friend to go out with for the day, so once in a partnership, Libra moons will do everything they can to maintain harmony and keep the peace. Ruled by the scales, compromise is not a problem at all, and if it means a quiet life and smiles all around, then they are happy to do so. Libra moons might give their partner a hug when they are upset or make soothing noises and sensible suggestions, but inside they hate it all—big time.

Raising their voice in anger is anathema to a Libra moon. They never argue back, which is for the best because they don't have loud voices. Libras speak in dulcet tones. "Surely," they will say, "this can be discussed quietly, calmly, and reasonably? There is no need to shout."

So partners be warned; no crying, no shouting, no anger. Too much of any of it and a Libra will move on. And if they decide to leave, they will very sweetly—and with great rapidity—extricate themselves. They are a cardinal sign, remember.

Libra always has an eye on beauty, peace, and harmony, and Libra moons seek this in their relationships. Even when in love, they make sensible choices and do not allow emotions to cloud their vision. They are quite apt to marry for money even though they are equally capable of working for their luxuries; they have an innate lazy streak and would much prefer someone else do all the hard work.

Libra moons enjoy all the trappings of love and romance: exotic holidays, luxury hotels, and being wined and dined. But they would rather draw a veil over the other, more mundane aspects of relationships. They are cerebral people, not physical. With a partner who provides enough luxury and comfort, they might exert themselves. But partners take note, Libra moons rarely enjoy the practical aspects of looking after others, so either do the household jobs yourself or employ staff.

## Moon in Scorpio (Fixed Water)

Scorpio moons play for keeps. They focus on one person and get the very most from their emotions: ups and downs, high drama, passionate emotions, deep sensitivity, and jealous suspicions. Scorpio is a deeply emotional water sign, and the moon in this sign needs to experience heightened emotion and passion, which makes for an exciting—and demanding—love life.

Scorpio moons enjoy playing cat and mouse. They are masters at mind games and manipulation, so they are adept at getting what they want in a subtle way. Two words describe Scorpio moons: control and passion. They keep a firm control over their own emotions and endeavour to control their partner. Once in love, Scorpio moons torment themselves with jealousy and suspicion. This is because they commit heart and soul, and once they have allowed themselves to trust someone, they know the pain they would feel if it all went wrong would be devastating. Their feelings run very, very deep.

Scorpio moons need to live life to the extreme and be pushed to their limits. While they prefer to focus on one person, if their relationship gets boring or too stuck in a routine, they will move on to new pastures. Scorpio moons need physical and emotional passion, and cosy comfort is of no interest to them.

Scorpio moons always hides their true motives behind a blank stare and a "couldn't care less" front. The stare isn't blank at all; it is laser-sharp, scanning and picking up psychic vibrations. It is almost impossible to lie to or mislead a Scorpio moon. Unless partners are interested in high drama and a passionate life, they should walk away.

If you don't mind being tested or watched and want to explore the highs and lows of life, all you need to do is take a leap into the dark, unfathomable depth of a Scorpio moon.

## Moon in Sagittarius (Mutable Fire)

Like all moon placements in fire signs, Sagittarius moons are warm and affectionate but cannot cope with overly emotional or needy people. Add to this mix that Sagittarians are renowned for their blunt honesty and it's possible to foresee their relationships might not always be easy. Their partner will have to be one tough cookie to take the brutal truth.

Sagittarius is the sign of a wanderer, both literally and mentally. Sagittarius moons have to feel unfettered and free to roam the world. They don't want to be tied down. With their irresistible need to explore and experiment, keeping to the straight and narrow will not appeal to them, nor is it feasible in reality.

A Sagittarius moon's ideal partner is someone who either willingly accompanies them on their adventures or who understands their need for personal freedom. It's also important that their partner understands that their desire to explore doesn't have anything to do with being unfaithful—but if an opportunity presents itself, they are the sign least likely to say no.

Sagittarius moons are highly adventurous, happy, and optimistic. They are great fun to have around. They never resort to manipulation because that requires subtlety and suspicion, neither of which are their forte.

Being a mutable sign, Sagittarius moons are quite capable of fitting in with the needs of others as long as it doesn't interfere with their own desires. They are, after all, a fire sign, and fire signs think of themselves first and others second.

How deeply a Sagittarius moon can be touched emotionally depends on a lot of other factors in their birth chart, so it would be wrong to say that they don't experience deep pain. However, it may appear this way because they are capable of shrugging off failures, chalking them up to experience, and moving on to the next great adventure.

### Moon in Capricorn (Cardinal Earth)

Capricorn moons are hard to please. Their partners need to be tidy, clean, and respectable. They won't look twice at someone who picks their teeth, sniffs, or drinks too much, and heaven forbid if the person swears or wears old clothes. It is a minefield pleasing a Capricorn moon! They want the very best in emotional terms. They are not about to give their hearts to someone who is dirty or disgusting, unclean or uncouth. That's because a Capricorn moon is going places: upward. And when they reach the pinnacle of their success, they want a partner who will not shame them in word or deed, so prospective partners need to brush up their act.

Emotionally, Capricorn moons are traditional. They are also very wary. Never in a million years will they be lured into a relationship with someone unsuitable. No matter how beautiful or handsome, no matter how alluring, if they don't have that certain something in their manner and dress, that elegance of style, Capricorn moons will not pursue them.

They don't want fast. They don't want a passing phase, a one-night stand, or even a brief fling. Capricorn moons want forever, and they will not waste their very valuable time on something that will not lead anywhere.

Because they intend to succeed in life, they will vet a potential partner's manners, bank balance, and family background. They must have no skeletons in their closet. Capricorn moons are aiming for success in their chosen profession, and if prospective partners want to come along, they need to get their act together—otherwise, the Capricorn moon will have become a millionaire while their ex-partner is stocking supermarket shelves.

## Moon in Aquarius (Fixed Air)

Air signs are all cool and detached in their emotional responses. Aquarius moons need mental stimulation and friendship more than wild passion.

Their partner is their link to the world. Without that bridge, Aquarius moons wander around in a sort of daze, not knowing quite what to do nor how to do it. They aren't socially adept at all, quite shy in fact, so while they have many friendships—and those, like their close relationships, are pursued out of curiosity and not because of a pressing need to relate to others in an emotional way—they need someone to hang on to who can show them the way things should be done. Aquarius moons will be there in person, but rarely in spirit.

Not only will their partners have to take on all the burdens of life, but they will have to be tolerant in the extreme. It is quite possible that an Aquarius moon might not come home one night. If they turn up in the morning calmly saying they stayed with a friend of the opposite sex, there is no need for jealousy—any interest in the opposite sex is unlikely to be for reasons of passion. It's more likely that they started a really interesting discussion and before they knew it, it was 4:00 a.m. Then the Aquarius moon will head to bed, leaving their long-suffering partner to handle the everyday tasks. There is no point getting angry. Aquarius moons are fixed. They are who they are, so take it or leave it.

Aquarius moons are an enigma. They walk around passionate encounters before embarking on them. Despite their intelligent, logical minds, they are still apt to take a chance on someone without really thinking it through, simply out of curiosity. They may end up married for the same reason. Then they'll spend years working out what makes their loved one tick. The only predictable thing about an Aquarian is that they are unpredictable.

Criticising Aquarius moons is a waste of time. Because they believe everyone is entitled to their opinion, they take nothing personally. They don't need to undermine anyone else to feel big, so they are excellent at guiding those less clever or just learning; they live and let live. But they expect the same in return. Independence and freedom of action are both essentials to an Aquarius moon. They need to feel a bit free sometimes. Let them wander off now and then; they will always come back because their sign is fixed. But it works both ways; they will allow their partners to have midnight cups of coffee with friends of the opposite sex.

Aquarians like to shock. Therefore, they often choose unusual partners. That covers just about anyone their friends and family might find surprising. There is only one rule with Aquarius moons: there are no rules.

### Moon in Pisces (Mutable Water)

As if the sign of Pisces isn't understanding enough, put the emotional moon here and you have the most gentle and compassionate person in the world. Being deeply vulnerable on an emotional level makes them understanding, sympathetic, and empathic toward others. No one is sweeter and kinder than a Pisces moon.

They make allowances all the time for the unforgivable behaviour of others, but just because they are soft does not mean they are stupid. They understand exactly how others are feeling, yet they have no way of helping other than with their soothing presence and kind words. They do not have the emotional strength to be all things to all people. If someone comes to them for help, they will make a cup of tea, pat their hand, allow them to unburden their worries as long as they like, then send them on their way.

Despite being such gentle people, Pisces moons are well-equipped to look after themselves, not in life—which they tend to muddle through—but emotionally. They know exactly the point when retreating is necessary for their own emotional well-being. When it's a matter of self-preservation, they can be surprisingly strong. For such a compassionate sign, Pisces moons are actually very cool and detached.

In relationships, they can be a bit of an enigma. They can love with deep devotion but often steer clear of relationships. Because they are easily hurt, tender, and kind, relationships are a bit of a minefield for them.

Pisces moons often seek a stronger partner who will protect them from the world. In marriage, Pisces moons are incredibly supportive spouses. They'll listen to their partner's moans about their terrible day with complete understanding and sympathy. They are also pretty easy to please; Pisces moons are touched by even the smallest of romantic gestures as long as they come from the heart.

Many Pisces moons are artistic or musical. They find that expressing their nature through music or an art form is far easier than putting their fluctuating moods and feelings into words.

# Mercury

**Affects:** Communication, speech, thought, mental faculties, how you think and communicate

In Roman mythology, Mercury is considered the messenger of the gods. In astrology, Mercury rules how we think and communicate. No matter what sun or moon signs a person has, the astrological sign Mercury is in when they are born will reflect how they think and communicate. Mercury rules the signs of Gemini and Virgo.

Look for Mercury's symbol in your chart. What astrological sign is it in? Then check the list of how it will work in each sign. Before reading the interpretations below, have a go at interpreting how you think Mercury works for you. Can you understand this aspect of yourself?

### Mercury in Aries (Cardinal Fire)

Mercury in Aries people are talkative and direct. Planets in Aries become assertive, and fast, remember? Their ideas come thick and fast. They will happily give anyone an idea for free, maybe even helping them set up a business, win over their crush, or plan their holiday. If someone else is as happy and enthusiastic about an idea as the Mercury in Aries person is, they won't expect to be paid. Even if they are in business, they will hand out free ideas and suggestions and offer their time to help out. Aries are warm-hearted and generous, and with this placement, it's their words and advice they willingly offer.

Mercury in Aries are pleasant, cheerful, trusting, and confiding. They are very talkative! However, a word of caution: They certainly do mean what they say—at the time. If others let the dust settle for too long on an idea or project, they will have moved on to new pastures. Act immediately and you have the attention of an Aries Mercury; delay and it is gone.

So, yes, they have a fund of ideas and can come up with any number of fun plans, but they are not the people to go into business with, not unless they are just the ideas person. Details are not their thing. Finances? Heavens, never leave a Mercury in Aries in charge of the money. They are generous and trusting and have no eye on the future.

Lastly, never tell a Mercury in Aries a secret. It is not that they are deliberately setting out to tell anyone (they really did not mean to), but in the midst of all their chatter, it somehow slipped out, leaving them mortified and upset. For a while, anyway.

### Mercury in Taurus (Fixed Earth)

Okay, let's be honest. This guy or gal isn't going to be setting the world on fire with their rhetoric. More likely, they will be monosyllabic—a grunt now and then, a hummed line from a song, the odd line like "What's for dinner?" Mercury, that winged communicator, crashes to earth in this steady, fixed sign. It cannot fly. It still works, of course, but at a slower pace. There is no point in speaking, Taurus thinks, when there isn't anything to say.

Taking time when making decisions means every angle has been thought out, every pitfall assessed, so that there is no room for error. That tends to mean a lack of vision, and Mercury in Taurus people are not renowned for their amazing ideas or incredible innovations. When a new idea is presented to them, they might need it explained to them more than once. It is not that they are not clever, but that it takes them a little longer to assimilate information.

Male Mercury in Taurus will be the strong, silent type; don't expect him to change his views or his mind. Female Mercury in Taurus appears calm and unruffled no matter what life throws her way. Like their male counterpart, they don't like change, especially when plans have been made to go somewhere and they are altered at the last minute. If you ask a female Mercury in Taurus to marry you and she says no, don't bother to ask again. She won't change her mind.

On the other hand, Taurus Mercury people are extremely reliable. If they've given a promise, it will be kept. If they agree to a meeting at a certain time, they will be there. They may not say much, but their word is their bond.

Expressing anger is not easy for them. They put up with a great deal before exploding. For years, others will think them cool, calm, steady, and uncomplaining, and then one day something happens that just takes them one step further than they are prepared to go—just wait for the fireworks! Their anger, once unleashed, is formidable. Best, then, not to push them too far. Accept that they are not going to change and that what you see is what you get.

## *Mercury in Gemini (Mutable Air)*

Mercury rules Gemini, so there is no better position for this planet of communication. Their minds are quick and agile, and they are capable of collecting and communicating a wide variety of knowledge. They are logical thinkers with interests that spread far and wide. They love to talk and exchange ideas. They absorb information, but very often it is superficial. That is why they make great raconteurs and speakers, being witty and amusing, but not good researchers. In-depth probing is not their style; they'll leave that to Mercury in Scorpio.

They often excel at sarcasm and cruel wit. It isn't personal—nothing Gemini does is personal—but they love the sheer joy of playing with words. It helps to have a thick skin and understand that they are simply having fun.

The modern world is a delight to them. Any and all forms of communication are avidly adopted; it's a sure thing they are the first people in the queue for the latest mobile phone. Well, make that the latest anything. They want to be where it's at, so it is a necessity for them to know all about the latest, most up-to-date advancement and to be the first to own it/use it.

They also take pleasure in modern culture. Celebrities are followed, gossip delighted in, fashion adopted as soon as it is on the high street. If they can appear on television they will—reality television was made for them! Radio is also of interest. Anywhere, in fact, that the written and spoken word is used for entertainment or information, you will find a Mercury in Gemini either directing proceedings or taking part.

Their Achilles' heel? Indecision. What they believe today, they won't believe tomorrow. Flexibility of thought is a great asset to any marriage or business, but when it comes to staying power? It has to be said, they don't have a good track record.

### Mercury in Cancer (Cardinal Water)

Anyone with Mercury in Cancer is receptive to others and makes a fabulous counselor. Planets in Cancer become emotional and protective, so it's not unusual for complete strangers to confide all sorts of personal information to a Cancer Mercury. Others feel in safe in their hands, and they are safe, because Cancer cares too much about people to ever be unkind or betray a confidence. Being so sensitive and vulnerable to pain gives them firsthand knowledge of the hurt they could inflict with any unkindness. They are great listeners, so people can unburden themselves to them in complete confidence. Mercury in Cancer really enjoys discussions about emotion and past hurts. These types of conversations reinforce their realisation that they are not alone; everyone has been rejected, betrayed, and wounded at some point in their life.

In any of the medical and care fields, there will be a liberal scattering of Mercury in Cancer people. There are so many things they can do, but the only thing they cannot do is live a life without thinking of others. They make good teachers and lecturers as long as it is a subject close to their hearts, personal, emotional, and of use. Nursing is a good example, but they are better psychologists and psychiatrists because when Mercury is in Cancer, it is the listening and talking aspects we are dealing with.

With this combination, Mercury in Cancer people do worry about things and are very sensitive to unkind words; a wayward remark can wound them deeply. Being so easily hurt, they need to take time out to retreat and recover, but being cardinal, very soon they have headed back out into the world to do what they do best: help others.

## *Mercury in Leo (Fixed Fire)*

Planets in Leo become bolder and more expressive, and fire signs like to talk about themselves anyway. It's just the way it is. Leo is ruled by the sun, after all, and is a regal sign. With Mercury here, they are likely to remind others of how brilliant they are now and then. Irritating as this might be, it is hard to get annoyed because they really are the best at what they do. Mercury in Leo people talk the talk but they also walk the walk. They are what it says on the tin. If they puff themselves up and declare they are fantastic, others can be quite sure they are. But it's no good saying nothing; Leo needs to be told how special they are. It is important that they know others appreciate them and their efforts.

Mercury in Leo people have a way with words. They want to sparkle and shine, to be in the spotlight. That is why they make great speakers—or perhaps I should say orators, because "speaker" does not do them justice. They are capable of passion and drama and rousing an audience. Shakespeare's Henry V probably had Mercury in Leo, the way he roused his battle-weary troops. Spurred on by his stirring words, the army attacked and won, and all because Henry had the ability to inspire and lead. That is what Mercury in Leo is capable of: inspiration and leadership. Even as children, people with Mercury in Leo will soon have their own willing group of followers who are prepared to do anything for their Leo leader.

Leos have good self-worth. With Mercury in Leo, it is their intellectual abilities they are proud of. They know they are smart, and they want to dominate the conversation. Glamorous ideas are very appealing to them—the grander the better. Better get someone else to attend to the details, though, because Leo doesn't do the small stuff.

Of course, there are negatives. Mercury in Leo does not like being told what to do. They are the bossy ones. They direct others. They might not roar in anger if approached carefully, but if you start an argument with them, they will win it by shouting the loudest. Fixed signs will never back down, but they will generously forgive and forget—as long as others admit they were wrong!

## *Mercury in Virgo (Mutable Earth)*

Planets in Virgo become practical and analytical. Anyone who knows anything at all about astrology will have heard that people born under the sign of Virgo are perfectionists. This is not a myth. Put Mercury, the planet of thought and communication, in this sign and we have the classic intellectual perfectionist.

Mercury in Virgo is the image of a jobsworth, the bureaucrat who drives everyone crazy with red tape they think is absolutely essential but which no one else can see the point of at all. Someone has to do it. Someone has to edit the magazines, critique restaurants, plan train and plane timetables, and work out how the latest city planning scheme should work. Someone has to be responsible for judging others. Look no further than a Mercury in Virgo as the perfect person for the job.

Mercury in Virgo people are in the background, busy and quietly and unassumingly tidying up messes and sorting out the details that no one else can be bothered with. They love order and a filing system. (The latter is in their heads.) Ask a Mercury in Virgo mother where their toddler's grey socks are and she'll know instantly (bottom drawer, right hand corner, under the blue shirt).

We can all see the positives in this, especially those fire signs that are dreaming up exciting schemes and leaving the details to someone else. It's almost as if Mercury in Virgo was invented just to tidy up after others, or to look after poor Mercury in Pisces who is busy being indecisive. What would Mercury in Gemini do without Mercury in Virgo reminding them of that meeting they need to attend or that the car is due for service?

They really are a godsend, these people—unless the train is due to leave in five seconds and they haven't got the right ticket. Similarly, a Mercury in Virgo official won't let anyone off easily if they don't have exactly the right documentation. Good luck trying to speed through customs if you're facing a Mercury in Virgo.

Living with them can be a bit stressful if friends and partners like scattering the newspapers on the floor and slopping soup down their front. Come to think of it, Virgo in Mercury wouldn't even be with them if they did that. It would upset them too much to be surrounded by disorder and mess, especially because they probably just spent two hours tidying up before their partner decided to toss the paper on the floor. If you take advantage of them too often, you're likely to get thrown out along with the newspaper and the soup-stained top!

## Mercury in Libra (Cardinal Air)

What a fabulous combination. Made in heaven! Mercury is the planet of communication, and Libra is an air sign. This is about as balanced as you can get.

It will come as no surprise that people with Mercury in Libra make incredibly good lawyers. Some are so clever with words it is hardly relevant if the criminal is guilty or not. They can effortlessly manipulate an audience with their rhetoric (or glibly lie if it suits their purpose), and they have an uncanny ability to turn situations around so their partner is to blame, but in such a subtle and astute way there is no arguing the point. Somehow, they will manage to justify everything without even raising their voices.

If they choose not to go into the law, they will still find a job that suits their talents perfectly. They are adept at bringing people together in a spirit of conciliation, so they make great mediators and counselors. They are good in human resources, too, having a way of fairly judging who would fit in with the team and who would upset the balance.

Sometimes they will be at their desk night and day. Then they will be off sick. They may not actually be ill, but they will certainly be worn out. Stamina is not their forte. For long periods of time they can work like beavers, then for an equally long period of time nothing will move them from those deep, soft cushions on the sofa.

But even if they look idle, their minds are working. Air signs think a lot. They put a lot of value on their intellectual processes, enjoying nothing more than long, complicated discussions where they can view a problem from every conceivable angle. So even if they are exhausted, others can always rouse them with a question about who is right or wrong in a disagreement.

When that light in their eye starts returning, everyone can breathe a sigh of relief. It won't be long before they are back at their desks.

## Mercury in Scorpio (Fixed Water)

No planet in the sign of Scorpio escapes without being fully used; Scorpio will drag every ounce of energy from it. People with this combination will have extremely powerful intellect, deep, incisive minds, and the courage to go where no one has gone before in terms of research and investigation. Their minds are penetrating and obsessive, capable of focussing on an idea until everything has been laid bare.

Their reactions and ideas are instinctive and intuitive and come from gut-feeling. Scorpio is a water sign, after all, emotional and deep, so their research will be driven by passion—a passion for the subject and the passion to be the one who finds the truth. Leaving no stone unturned, they make excellent researchers and detectives. Not only are they incisive and sharp, they are intuitive—often psychic—and very, very clever.

But others won't see this. Outwardly, Scorpio will look unconcerned, uninterested, and blasé. They like to be in control, and they start with themselves. They are not about to let other people know how much a project means to them or how many hours they've spent researching and planning.

They don't like being answerable to anyone else, that is for sure, because they do not believe anyone else has their cleverness or ability, not even their boss. They are only biding their time before taking over, anyway.

Scorpio does everything in secret until they have come up with answers. Then they think about how to best present information so it reflects well on them and brings them the greatest rewards. Nothing is rushed or hasty, and they don't gossip or chat endlessly about nothing. They play their cards close to their chests, but it is not a game to Scorpio. Nothing is a game. Everything is serious and meaningful, and they intend to win—or at least to come out smelling of roses.

No one else's opinion is of the least interest to a Scorpio Mercury. They might pretend to listen politely, but their sign is fixed, which means once they have made up their minds, nothing will shift them.

Unusual subjects appeal to them. The more mysterious, the deeper their interest. Even if they don't delve into it themselves, they will accept the words of those who are psychic or clairvoyant because they know there is more out there than is visible to the naked eye. They won't like it, though; Scorpio likes to remain an enigma, and if they think someone might actually be able to read their mind rather than the other way around, it makes them edgy.

They believe the end justifies the means, so Mercury in Scorpio people can lie or mislead others quite easily if they are backed into a corner but don't want to reveal anything. No sleep will be lost over it, either.

There is something unusual about the voices of people with this combination; they are different in some way. Regardless, they usually make excellent public speakers.

## Mercury in Sagittarius (Mutable Fire)

Sagittarians are natural philosophers and constant seekers of the truth. Different religions, cultures, and languages fascinate them and most will make study a lifelong passion, moving from one subject to another with equal interest.

While a Sagittarius Mercury is in the throes of enthusiasm about something, get them to a meeting and ask them to speak. They actually make very good orators while they are still fascinated by a subject. They also have a blunt but straight sense of humour and can be hilarious. Being so versatile in their interests, they usually have a good supply of stories for gatherings. As a fire sign they are quick, mentally agile, and intuitive.

Honesty is their best trait, but hurting people is not their style, so they are surprised when others are upset by their remarks. Like all Mercury fire signs, they don't give much forethought to their speech. It's easy for them to unintentionally traipse all over someone's tender heart without even realising it.

Their minds are active and searching, and they are constantly coming up with new ideas. Hardly have they finished telling everyone about one idea before the next is lining up. It would be unusual for Mercury in Sagittarius not to have at least three or four projects going on at the same time.

Details are their stumbling block. Stop them mid-flow and ask a detailed question and they will lose track of what they were saying. They do ideas and enthusiasm, not fact and figures. Ask a Mercury in Virgo for those!

## Mercury in Capricorn (Cardinal Earth)

Planets in Capricorn become pragmatic and cautious. These people think. *Really* think. They do not rush matters, but what they come up with is certainly worth listening to. Yes, it might be a tad on the dull side, maybe a bit old-fashioned even, but in Capricorn's mind it worked then and it will work now. They are not interested in newfangled, unproven ideas. A quick buck is not their style. And they never make a mistake. If they say something will work or is worth thinking about, believe them. It might mean waiting for a bit to see the returns and rewards, but rest assured, they will come.

In relationships? Well, let's just say they are not about to set the world on fire with their interesting chatter. They think a lot, then say something. More likely, they do something. Mercury in Capricorn people take sensible and reasoned actions. Maybe their partner has been moaning about that neighbour who keeps letting his dog bark half the night and the students who rent that house nearby who have noisy parties until the early hours. A Capricorn Mercury will listen but may not immediately respond; they can be incredibly tolerant. But when their partner is on the edge of knocking down a few doors in exhausted anger, a Capricorn Mercury will make the noise stop. First they make sure the disturbing noise is not a passing phase and then contact the correct authorities, who look into it (in their own time, as they do). Finally, peace descends. No angry confrontations, no hassle, just peace. Thank you, Capricorn Mercury.

Next, hand them the finances. As they never look at quick ways of making money, long-term investments will be their forte, but in their capable hands it's guaranteed that nest egg will grow to a substantial size in thirty years (or more). Trustworthy, reliable, safe? Without a doubt. But quick? Capricorn does not know or understand that word. One day others will appreciate Capricorn Mercury's advice more than they can know.

### Mercury in Aquarius (Fixed Air)

Mercury is how we think and communicate. Planets in Aquarius become erratic, free, and unpredictable, so here we have someone whose thoughts and ideas are forward-thinking, unusual, and quite likely verging on genius.

These are the people who have always thought outside the box. These are the Nobel Prize winners for incredible breakthroughs in science and medicine. These are the groundbreaking thinkers who quite naturally function at a different intellectual level than the rest of us.

Okay, so maybe they are not all going to make the big time. Quite frankly, they don't care. Material possessions are not even on their radar. Neither is fame and fortune. To be truthful, most Aquarius Mercury people are so wrapped up in their latest invention that someone else will probably get the patent before them. Mercury in Aquarius forgot that someone else might get there first. Even if that happens, they won't mind much because they have no personal feelings of animosity or jealousy. They'll just move on to the next project. It's all about their curiosity and finding answers to their questions. Success or failure do not matter to them.

They will be interesting speakers. And yes, that was facetious. It will be unlikely that a Mercury in Aquarius will have written anything down or made any plans of what they intend to say. They wing it. This means they may be incredible and funny and wise, or they may be dreadful, so bad that everyone is squirming in embarrassment. Either way, they don't give a fig. They have no interest in what other people think or how they look or what's going on outside their own thought processes. In fact, they are quite shy, but not so shy they can't stand in front of an audience and talk about what excites them the most.

They wish to help in a detached, impersonal, universal sort of way, so any invention that furthers mankind will appeal greatly. But it has to be said they are better at coming up with ideas and leaving others to deal with the practicalities. That will leave them free to wait for the next brainwave.

## Mercury in Pisces (Mutable Water)

Clairvoyants, psychics, and mediums often have this combination. Quite frankly, it isn't of much use in the technical or mathematical world because Mercury loses all of its logic when in the sign of Pisces, yet all the intuitive channels are open. They just know. How do they know? That they won't be able to explain. They just *do*.

So why is it that Mercury in Pisces produces this? Well, Pisces is a water sign, and water is intuitive. Mercury is the opposite; it is logical and clearheaded. Immerse it in water and it's like dunking a biscuit in hot liquid—it disintegrates. All the logic dissipates and you are left with only instinct and intuition.

To put it another way, imagine putting your head under muddy water. Without being able to hear or see clearly, how can you find your way? Mercury in Pisces lives in this underwater world, so it is no surprise that they think in a vague, dreamy, confused way. To do anything at all, they have to tune in to intuition. Consequently, they dislike making decisions, and even when they do, they are never quite sure if it was the right one. It is obvious that jobs that require an organised, logical mind will be an impossibility for Mercury in Pisces.

Logic holds no interest to them, but they do find concepts fascinating. Physicists, for example, use mathematics to explain their theories. Pisces will ignore the figures but talk for hours about the concepts, and astutely at that. Just because they aren't logical and can't make fast decisions does not mean they are stupid. Oh no, they are very clever, only not in the same way everyone else is clever. Our world bases intelligence on being able to learn by rote and produce facts and figures. Mercury in Pisces may not be much good at that, but they understand things on a far deeper and more complicated level. They can commune with different worlds and tune in to unseen vibrations. So why would they be interested in a few facts and figures when they see all of life from an entirely different perspective? Anyway, everyone knows facts and figures can be manipulated.

In real life, though, Mercury in Pisces can appear muddled. To remind themselves of things, they write endless lists, then forget to take the lists with them. They'll start talking about something and then lose the thread halfway through, and they will change their minds a thousand times over the tiniest of decisions.

But people shouldn't laugh because they are so hopelessly fuzzy with details. When life knocks someone down, it will be a Pisces Mercury who helps them pick up the pieces and suggests the one thing that is guaranteed to get them back on track. On top of that, a Mercury in Pisces will listen for hours, make them a cup of tea, and give them a loan to help them on their way.

# Venus

**Affects:** Love, harmony, artistic sense, appreciation of beauty, how you love

Venus is the planet of love. It seeks harmony and balance. The astrological sign it is in when we are born shows how we love and whether we compromise with partners or prefer to take charge of our relationships. Venus rules the signs of Taurus and Libra.

Find the symbol for Venus in your birth chart. What astrological sign is it in? Taking into account its element and motivation, can you relate to it? Check below to see how accurate your predictions were. Are you getting the hang of predicting how planets act in signs?

## *Venus in Aries (Cardinal Fire)*

So, Venus in Aries. Venus is love, is it not? The planet of love should be gentle, loving, warm, and caring. Hmm. Well, Aries is warm!

Venus in Aries is direct. Very direct. No beating about the bush, no gentle flirting, no nuances. With Aries, it is straight to the point. Both men and women will go right up to the one they like and say so. They will invite them out and give a time and place. If the object of their desire is elusive, shy, or even a tad unsure, they will move on. They will not waste time wooing and playing those little romantic games. They are honest and cannot see the point of wasting time on long, drawn-out romantic foreplay.

Venus in Aries women can take your breath away with their directness. Men just seem more confident and surer than most. Either way, romance is not their forte. "We like each other, so let's get on with it" is their reasoning.

They enjoy being in love because they are warm and affectionate. Being so generous means their loved one is treated well, with no thought to cost when it comes to enjoyment. But Venus in Aries people are useless at compromise and they positively loathe emotional scenes, so partners need to be tough enough to handle all their own emotional issues. Venus in Aries will give them a quick hug, offer a word of advice, and then head off to do something. They are independent and expect partners to deal with their own problems.

If it doesn't work out, Venus in Aries can move on. They are not unfeeling, but being cardinal fire, they act positively by looking for someone new. There will be no emotional drama, no lengthy discussions, just a straight to the point "This is not working, I'm off" conversation, and away they go! There is no intention of hurting someone else with this bluntness because Venus in Aries don't have a mean bone in their bodies; it is just an acceptance that the end has come. Quite refreshing, really.

## *Venus in Taurus (Fixed Earth)*

It has to be said, this fixed earth sign values possessions and money. Heaven for them means a healthy bank balance in a prospective partner. They will already have savings and a steady job, so there is no way they will fall for a fly-by-night who will run through their hard-earned savings; they simply aren't drawn to those who are lazy and unproductive. They choose partners who are keen to settle, who want to build a lasting—ideally, permanent—relationship. If they meet someone who is conservative and sensible, who saves their money, who has a house (or intends to get one), and who wants to marry and have children, it is possible they will make a commitment. But they will consider long and hard first. No way do they want to put in years of effort and have nothing to show for it at the end. They build. Falling for a Venus in Taurus? Build along with them.

Once emotionally committed, Venus in Taurus can put up with a lot from their partners, whom they prefer to be as calm as they are. If they pick someone who suddenly gets emotional, they might stand back a bit and think, *Whoa, this is scary.* But, as long as the dust settles without recourse to calling an ambulance, they will shrug and get on with it. Once Venus in Taurus has committed to a person, it takes many years of bad treatment for them to move on.

In fact, Venus is ideally placed here. Taurus brings out all the earthy, steady qualities in Venus and provides the perfect setting for stable, loving relationships. It also means a love of the sensuous; they love to touch, make love, eat good food, enjoy fine wines, and visit luxury hotels. Consequently, they do make very good partners because they are conscious of another's welfare and comfort. They are keen to provide a warm, loving, secure atmosphere at home, and they accept the good along with the bad.

But—it has to be said—Venus in Taurus lovers are possessive. They view their partner as "theirs" as much as their house and land. If their partner walks out, the first thing they feel is disbelief, then confusion. Why would they leave when Venus in Taurus gave them everything? An empty house is heartbreak for Taurus. They want to share a nice meal, snuggle up on the sofa, and have sex. After a time of immobility—because they will need time to absorb this new situation—they will start again, shoring up this part of their edifice by finding another partner.

Because they hate change, Venus in Taurus tries very hard to make relationships work, even when it is obvious they are doomed. Being fixed earth, they like continuity, so they bend over backward to salvage a failed relationship, especially if their standard of living will be affected as well. Love, to them, is the uniting of the physical with the financial, and they need both to really blossom.

## Venus in Gemini (Mutable Air)

Gemini is an air sign and as such, Venus in Gemini needs to move freely, without constraint. It connects through communication, so they will first be attracted to mental rapport. If Gemini can talk naturally and openly with someone who shares their ideas and love of excitement and change, they may fall in love.

However, be warned. Venus in Gemini may seem interested, then disappear to chase another rainbow, leaving you high and dry. They may even make a date, only to not show up. Very often, after they have declared their love, they actually *do* disappear for a while, which gives them a bit of space to consider the new whirling emotions inside.

Venus in Gemini doesn't like whirling emotions; they don't like emotions, full stop. Emotions cloud things. Geminis like their independence and to keep a clear head. If a Venus in Gemini has other personal planets in earth signs, they may well come back and continue the relationship, but prospective partners must be very careful not to push for commitment or settling down together. Commitment should come from Gemini. It should be their idea, otherwise they are likely to disappear again—and this time permanently. So, no, they are not easy to pin down.

Gemini is the sign of the twins, so there are two people to please. Venus in Gemini easily moves from one to the other. Very often, one twin is the "good guy" and the other is bad. Not that Gemini does anything *that* bad; the bad Gemini is more likely to be irritable, snappy, and critical. Geminis do wit and sarcasm very well, so if they have moved from the nice twin—the one who is fun and exciting—to being judgmental about someone's clothes or being sarcastic, all that's happened is they have moved to the other twin, their alter ego. Wait a while and the nice one will come back; they come as a package.

That is about as bad as Venus in Gemini will get, because they believe that life is too short for all that emotional stuff; crying, bullying, demanding, or possessive behaviour just scares them off. Passion is another thing they don't really do. Their love is more cerebral than physical, and they are unlikely to indulge in dramatic displays of affection or passionate love-making (not unless they have a planet or two in Scorpio, Taurus, or Virgo).

They do, of course, marry and settle—sort of. Most Geminis have more than one marriage. They have double of everything—at least one for each twin—so it is better to catch them the second time around. In truth, most Venus in Gemini people don't settle when they are young anyway, so by the time they do, they may have exhausted all other possibilities and be quite ready to stay put. For a while. If they have stayed with one partner all their lives, you can be pretty sure their birth chart has some planets in earth signs.

Boredom kills a relationship for a Gemini. If you keep the spark alive and the interest going and give them plenty of space, they could very well be the most charming and cultured of partners. They aren't looking for someone to play house with, but for a partner who looks good at parties and makes sparkling conversation—just like them, in fact. Venus in Gemini people are attracted to partners who are inventive with date ideas, provide input, make suggestions, and drop a few pithy quotes into the conversation now and then. Basically, don't sit there all evening moaning about the weather or staring blankly at the television if you want to attract a Venus in Gemini. Make lively conversation!

### Venus in Cancer (Cardinal Water)

Oh, love! Don't we all love being in love? Venus in Cancer does. When they are adored, it makes them feel safe; it feels like everything is right with the world. Surely, this person who is declaring undying love would never hurt them? Surely, they can come out of their shells and relax and give this person their entire heart in return?

Let's hope so. Let's hope they trusted the right person. Being intuitive, they are usually pretty good at determining whom they can trust, because for Venus in Cancer people, trusting is a very brave thing to do. They are so deeply sensitive to pain that trusting someone else is a daring leap of faith. But they know that in order to gain the security in love that they so desperately need, some-where along the line they have to take a chance.

Venus in Cancer people aim to surround themselves with the security of a loving family who will never cause them hurt and who will protect them from the cold, harsh world—or at least the unfeeling, unkind people who inhabit it, whom Cancer always seems to meet. The sign of Cancer is the crab, and their family is their shell.

Once they have their family—and it may take them some time to have children because they worry they won't make a good enough parent—they will create a lovely home; cosy and comfortable, with home-cooked food, bedtime stories, and lots of love. A harmonious home life is very important to them, as is a reliable and trustworthy partner. They don't mind working hard outside the home, either, as long as they can go back to the emotional security of their family unit.

If their marriage fails, they will cling on a long time after the writing is on the wall. They, more than most (except perhaps Taurus), can tolerate a less-than-perfect situation for the sake of the children or for financial considerations. Being without money in the bank is almost as hard to deal with as being without love, but at least with rainy day money they can find a cosy place to retreat to and lick their wounds. To desert their family, they would have to be under extreme duress; it is not something they would ever lightly undertake because their guilt would haunt them forever.

### Venus in Leo (Fixed Fire)

Romance with a capital R, that's a Leo Venus. Warm, affectionate, and loving, they adore all things to do with love and romance. But it has to be said, they like the best in life, so classy restaurants and exotic holidays heighten their desire. In the right place, with a nice meal and a few drinks, Venus in Leo will soon be in love. Half of their emotions will be focused on their date, the other half on the love of life itself. They will sit at a table, sipping wine and watching the sun set over the ocean, and just sigh with delight. Everything is right with the world when Leo feels loved and loves in return. Add some luxury and you'll have one happy pussycat.

Venus in Leo will dress to impress, go to the best places, enjoy the finest wines, and act like a Hollywood star. They want to be one of the beautiful people. Even if they have quite ordinary lives, they are adept at pretending. Just for those few hours, they can make-believe they have it all. Go along with them, rise to the occasion, and who knows where love might lead?

Very few Venus in Leos forget birthday presents. And do not ever forget theirs. That is a cardinal sin in their eyes—they should be the centre of their partner's world. Given the right amount of attention, they are very affectionate and loving, but no one should attempt to usurp their position as top dog or forget those little attentions.

If love ends, it is hard for Venus in Leo to accept. The fixity of the sign doesn't like change, but the worst part is knowing the one they loved prefers another. This is hell for them. They are so proud they cannot imagine their partner finding anyone as good as them or admiring someone else. The damage it does to their self-esteem is immense.

They can get bossy and a little conceited, but no one is warmer, more full of life, and more aglow with animal magnetism than Venus in Leo when they are loved and admired.

### Venus in Virgo (Mutable Earth)

The main problem with Venus in Virgo is actually getting them into a relationship in the first place. They are so difficult to please that one wonders if there is anyone at all who would suit them.

Venus in Virgo thinks long and hard before they even commit to a date. Is the prospective partner clean, respectable, and preferably a bit old-fashioned? They won't tolerate loud, noisy, brash types and hate to be shown up in public. They will also expect their partners to know which knife and fork to use, to not talk with their mouth full, and to wear nice, uncreased clothes.

However, let's assume these tests have been passed, otherwise Venus in Virgo won't accept (or offer) a date. Let's assume someone has actually managed to get one of these cool customers into a relationship. They are pleasantly surprised by Virgo's attention: have they eaten, do they need their clothes ironed, have they got the project ready for the next day? Venus in Virgo will take them breakfast in bed and are, under their icy exterior, more passionate than once realised. They look after their partners and are generally amenable. Venus in Virgo people hate to say no, even if they want to, so they tend to go along with their partner's ideas, and as long as their partner keeps themselves and their surroundings clean and tidy, Virgo is pretty nice to be around.

If the partner of a Venus in Virgo doesn't comply with the above, Virgo simply cannot help pointing out their faults, of which (they have now discovered) there are many. Funny how they thought they were brilliant before Venus in Virgo came along. But no, they leave the toothpaste top off, the toilet seat up, the bath mat all screwed up, the breakfast dishes unwashed, and the car's tank on empty. Pick any subject and Venus in Virgo will easily find fault because it's the things we all do that irritate them most.

Venus in Virgo won't give up on their partner, though, because they are destined to find fault anywhere and everywhere, and if isn't their current partner, it will be their next love. Eventually, Venus in Virgo comes to realise that as no one is without fault, they might as well take what is on offer and learn to live with it.

If Venus in Virgo wakes up one day to find that their partner actually does have feet of clay but is trapped because of children or finances, their bitterness will become so great that the constant criticisms will break up the best of relationships and send the most steadfast of partners running for cover. However, if partners meet their exacting standards, Venus in Virgo make very good lifelong mates.

A female Venus in Virgo is loyal, willing to help if it aids another, uncomplainingly taking on children, responsibilities from previous liaisons, and elderly parents. She will cook, iron, and clean up for the whole household as well as do her day job. In return, she will need a lot of reassurance that her sacrifices are appreciated.

Male Venus in Virgo is not an easy man to please. He could spend a lot of time nitpicking and getting hung up on what seem to be mere details. He will bring any aggravation at the office home with him; he'll worry about it, talk about it, fret about it, and lose some sleep over it. He needs a calm, understanding partner to soothe away his worries. Like female Venus in Virgos, he will be inclined to criticise his partner. But, also like his female counterpart, he will be loyal and trustworthy. He will take on the responsibilities of past liaisons, elderly mothers, decrepit dogs, and all the general emotional baggage that comes along with new partners. He may retreat to his study now and then, but he will appear for meals looking calm, unruffled, and as if he hasn't a care in the world.

Venus in Virgo people are like swans, sailing smoothly along on the waters of life, but if you look closer, you'll see their little legs going nineteen to the dozen underneath.

### Venus in Libra (Cardinal Air)

Romance? Oh yes! Venus rules Libra, so this is a perfect match. Libra adores romance. To them, romance is a luxury hotel, champagne, designer clothes, and being seen in all the right places with someone stunning on their arm. This really matters to them. They want life to be pleasant, beautiful, calm, and without any blemish—just like them, in fact, because they are all gorgeous individuals, blessed with a dimple or two, tender eyes, and fine skin. Nothing would please them more than a world full of beautiful people living a dreamy existence of harmony and peace.

Male Venus in Libra people will have tousled hair and come-to-bed eyes just as much as the females, but when it comes to actually doing anything physical … well, let's just say Scorpio does passion better and then draw a veil over that part—which is what Venus in Libra would like to do. If their partner is clean, romantic, tender, and gentle, they might quite like sex, but on the whole, it's a very basic, animalistic activity, and Venus in Libra isn't really into that. Still, if it means a candlelit meal on a terrace with champagne and some other beautiful people, it might be a price worth paying.

Libra is the sign of partnership, so Venus in Libra people do not feel whole on their own. As long as their partner is kind and generous, they will tolerate quite a lot in order to be part of a twosome. They will bend over backward to compromise and let partners have what they want if it keeps the peace, but they know when to draw the line. If they think their partner is being totally unfair, they will say so. They won't shout or rage because they have quiet voices. But, remember, they are a cardinal sign, so they will take action if they are unhappy. The end will come suddenly. It might come in a sweetly worded email or text, or Venus in Libra might just disappear one day. Like everything else they do, avoiding unpleasantness is key, so they will take the option that offers a quiet escape with no emotional scenes.

This sign, above all others, is more than happy to marry for money. Although quite capable of making their own way in life, the more cushioned they are from reality, the more they feel safe and relaxed. And when they feel safe, they can create a home life that is a haven of peace from the rigours of outside life.

## Venus in Scorpio (Fixed Water)

Prospective partners be warned! If you have a fireproof nature, are used to being constantly tested in love, and can deal with outpourings of emotion, lots of drama, and being controlled and possessed, it's game on.

Scorpio is an emotional water sign, which means they live by their emotions and intuitive gut instincts, so even Venus, the delightful planet of love, gets embroiled in their tangled desires. Venus in Scorpio people live for love. Not the love of many, but the love of one. The chosen one. Scorpio believes in fate, in twin souls. When they find that special person, they will leave no stone unturned to secure them and bring them into their lives. And a Scorpio on a mission is unstoppable. They don't take no for an answer, and they know how to seduce and beguile and tempt others.

Once Venus in Scorpio has the object of their affection, the intensity does not end there. Oh no. They don't like boredom and the easy life. Sitting together cosily on the sofa is not their style. They like passion all the time, so if their relationship is getting dull, they liven things up a bit by throwing in a challenging word or a jealous suspicion and the roller coaster starts up again. Their partner might groan, but Scorpio has their attention, so life is fun again.

Scorpio, no matter how giving they may appear, always takes care of number one first and foremost. Something must come back to them for their efforts. After that, they don't mind being generous. But they are so subtle in their manipulation of people and situations, partners may not even realise how much in control of the relationship—and of them—Venus in Scorpio is.

Partners should not even consider glancing in the direction of someone of the opposite sex. A chance remark about another person's good looks could spark all sorts of trouble. Scorpio has to be top dog, so all they've done is opened a can of worms. If their partner laughs and declares it was only a joke, too late! The damage has been done. Venus in Scorpio will test and retest their partner to make sure they really aren't thinking of going off with someone else. It is impossible to say in exactly what way their partner will be tested, but it will take many forms and turn them inside out. And just because they commented on someone's good looks! Imagine what could happen if their partner actually had the temerity to be unfaithful. It's not advisable.

There is something about a Venus in Scorpio person that is worth all this hassle and drama. No one will love as deeply, as fully, as passionately. This is someone who will fight their partner's battles, protect them, love them like no other, and defend them to the death. To have all this, maybe it is worth putting up with the constant suspicion, jealousy, and control issues? Well, that's your decision!

### Venus in Sagittarius (Mutable Fire)

If you are looking for someone lighthearted and carefree who won't tie you down, this is the ideal partner. Venus in Sagittarius finds it hard to settle in one relationship for long because the new and exciting appeals to them. They don't do long-term, nor do they like routine. Freedom is a necessity—freedom to come and go and to love whomever they feel inclined to at any particular moment. They might be very settled individuals in other areas of their life, but with Venus in this sign, they are not settled when it comes to love.

The trouble is, Venus in Sagittarius people are so exciting and interesting that it's hard for others to resist them. Anyone with a touch of Sagittarius in their chart has been to lots of places and done many things, so it is hardly surprising that they make such interesting companions. They can talk for hours about what they have done, are about to do, or would like to do. How can others not get caught up in their enthusiasm?

However, listen carefully. Make sure those dreams actually do include another person. If you are wide-eyed in anticipation, already imagining yourself trekking in the Himalayas or riding camels in the Gobi Desert, you might not hear the "I" instead of "we." In other words, be careful to distinguish whether Venus in Sagittarius is dreaming about their own future or planning the trip as a couple. They are blunt to the point of cruelty, but not to deliberately wound. They just say it exactly how it is. So they are quite likely to say, "Oh, I didn't mean *we* were going to Africa. I meant *me*. Alone."

If you are equally interesting and can throw in a few exciting place names and holiday destinations, you may get more than a spark of interest from

Venus in Sagittarius. You might even get that invitation after all! But never forget that once the trip ends and they are back home, Venus in Sagittarius is quite likely to flit off somewhere else while you are busy searching for a nice, cosy flat to share.

To be a part of the life of a Venus in Sagittarius, you must be ready to go anywhere at a moment's notice, to talk for hours about obscure subjects, to sleep on floors or under the stars, to find your pockets empty (money is the last thing they think of), and to have the most exciting and adventurous life it is possible to have. Even better, if you have the cash to finance the next expedition, you may be able to hold on to your wandering star!

## *Venus in Capricorn (Cardinal Earth)*

Venus in an earth sign is all about longevity. Earth signs don't like to play and have fun. Earth signs want to build. Earth signs like long-term, and none more so than Capricorn. But it will not be easy to turn the head of this new love, not if they have a Capricorn Venus. They are looking for a class act. If someone is a bit of a slob and likes lounging around in their pyjamas all day, Venus in Capricorn won't even look in their direction. They like smartly dressed people, and that means suits.

Yes, even in this day and age, there is nothing like a smart designer suit to light the spark of romance in the eyes of a Capricorn Venus. To lure a Capricorn man, wear a little black dress, but for heaven's sake, no cleavage, no bingo wings, no undyed roots showing. Be decorous, be demure, be old-fashioned. Prospective partners must use their napkin, be polite, know which knife and fork to use (yes, Capricorns still care about this), and know how to make small talk. One day they will need all these social graces because Venus in Capricorn is going places, and if you want to tag along, that is the price to pay. Believe me, it will be worth it.

Venus in Capricorn people are not above marrying for money and status. Anything that takes them a step higher in life is a plus. Of course, their intended partner does have to come up to the mark. No matter how rich, the above applies. They simply cannot love someone untidy, unclean, or uncouth. This sounds mercenary, and yes, it is, but they will not use and then dump their partner. A Capricorn Venus will stay around forever.

Romance? You bet! Remember those old films where the man drove miles to see his new love with flowers and an engagement ring in his pocket? That's the Capricorn way: traditional. They won't want to leap into bed on the first date, nor will they propose quickly. Capricorn Venus women want old-fashioned romance: flowers, a proper engagement, a white wedding, the required number of children, if possible. They want what grandma had, as well as all the other generations before. They like the way things have always been done. Ditto for Capricorn Venus men. Nothing turns them off more than a prospective partner taking the lead.

Capricorns are not flighty. Want excitement? Venus in Aries, Gemini, and Sagittarius are here today, gone tomorrow guys and gals. Want forever? Choose Venus in Capricorn.

### Venus in Aquarius (Fixed Air)

The main problem with Venus in Aquarius is getting them interested in love in the first place. *What is love?* they ask themselves as they scratch their heads. However, they, like the rest of us, do like companionship, so they will launch themselves into the world and hope some passing stranger takes pity on them.

They don't make the first move, and when someone else does, they will be momentarily surprised. If the prospective partner is different in some way, Venus in Aquarius may be interested. It is impossible to determine in what way partners need to be different because there is no understanding the Aquarian mind. They don't understand their own motivations, so how can anyone else hope to? Venus in Aquarius people don't know what it is they are looking for, but they will know it when they see it. Yet, they are still capable of letting the moment pass them by and losing what could have been a really lovely partnership. So, rule number one is, prospective partners must make the first move—and the second and the third and so on.

If a partner is willing and able to take on a Venus in Aquarius for life, they must plan the wedding, make all the arrangements, and assign someone reliable to make sure the Venus in Aquarius is there on time and in suitable clothes. The latter is particularly important because Aquarians like to stand out from the crowd by being unconventional. In modern day, this isn't as easy as it used to be. Now that anything goes, more or less, they find it harder to shock—hence the need for that reliable and trustworthy person to guide them to the place of the ceremony and making sure they are suitably attired. This applies to men and women.

Now that they've made a commitment, how will they be as a partner? Well, they do not tend to feel deep, passionate emotions. They don't go in for demonstrative displays of their affections, and dramatic emotional scenes are a no-no. They don't understand the concepts of jealousy and manipulation. This may make their partners feel unappreciated, which may lead to questions about how much they love them, which will lead to Venus in Aquarius walking out the door for a while.

But they usually come back. Aquarius is a fixed sign, so they don't like change. Apart from that, who else would care for them like their partner does? However, they need personal freedom and can't abide being trapped anywhere. Back them into a corner and they will escape for a while, and then nothing will have been achieved.

Venus in Aquarius cannot be what they aren't. And they aren't dramatic, passionate, or emotional. They love in their own cool, calm, detached sort of way, and to expect more is batting your head against a brick wall. No amount of crying or shouting is going to change a thing.

The sign of Aquarius is interested in humanity as a whole and rarely understands people on a personal level. What they ideally seek is a friend. Friendships, they understand those. Mental compatibility is high on their list.

If Venus in Aquarius decides they like someone, they don't give a hoot what anyone else thinks. Being an unpredictable sign, they might suggest marriage right there and then. Best you don't refuse, because they might just wander off. Tie the knot while you can, but be prepared to allow Aquarius plenty of room to breathe and roam—and accept that you will take on pretty much all the responsibilities. In return, you'll have someone who gives you plenty of personal freedom, will never get jealous when you choose to go on holiday with your friends, and who will never seek to change you.

### Venus in Pisces (Mutable Water)

This is the gentlest and most susceptible of all the signs when it comes to love. It is a fact of life that strong, forceful people like the company of soft, gentle people. Therefore, both men and women with Venus in Pisces are an accident waiting to happen in romantic terms. It is easy to tread on their tender hearts; people do it all the time. Not intentionally, but because our world is not a gentle place and Venus in Pisces are deeply sensitive and romantic.

Venus in Pisces finds it almost impossible to stand up for themselves or to argue a point. They understand human nature—they take it into account and see every point of view as valid—so how can they defend their own as any better?

They are loving, sympathetic, and self-sacrificing, and nothing is too much trouble when it comes to those they love. Their partners and children will be adored. Okay, so the house may be a bit messy, the garden chaotic, and the meals a bit random, but when it comes to feelings, there is no lack of love in their household. *And after all*, they reason, *isn't love more important than a tidy bedroom?* As for finances, well, let's just assume their stronger partner has that bit sorted.

In order to survive in an ordered, fast-paced world, Pisces has to pull out all the stops. They run themselves ragged, and they are easily tired. They really do try to be all things to all people, but people's demands are never-ending and Venus in Pisces simply can't do as much as they would like. They would willingly take on everyone's burdens and the sorrow of the world to protect others if they could, but they can't. They feel so deeply that they are drained by even one person's problems. And there is no end to people's problems. *Why*, they wonder, *can't everyone just love each other and live and let live?*

It is easy to love a Venus in Pisces. How can you not? They are romantic in the extreme and generous to a fault with their time and money. Venus in Pisces will follow your dreams, allow you to be who you are, and support you 100 percent. In return, you should always remember how sensitive Pisces is. Now and then, stop and ask them about their dreams. It would be great if you tried to fulfil one or two. Pisces goes through a thousand pains for others, so it's hardly much to ask in return, is it?

# Mars
## ♂

**Affects:** Assertiveness, forcefulness, activity, decisiveness, sex, war, anger, response to challenges, life force, drive

Mars is the planet of ambition and assertion. It is life force and drive. It shows what a person is driven to seek in life. The astrological sign it is in shows what motivates and inspires a person. Mars rules the sign of Aries.

## Mars in Aries (Cardinal Fire)

Wow, who was that whirlwind that just came by? That faster-than-light person, the one who was smiling broadly, shaking hands, and talking to everyone as if they were old friends? The one who only stayed twenty minutes and has now gone, leaving the room less warm and bright in their absence? That was Mars in Aries. Men and women alike light up a room with their energy and enthusiasm, their sparkle and warmth. Then they are off, heading on to the next exciting meeting, project, or holiday. Catch their coattails if you can!

Out of ideas? No problem. Mars in Aries has loads. One at a time, to be sure, but plenty of them. If one idea doesn't work, a new one will soon come along to lift their enthusiasm. Depression? What's that? Mars in Aries does not do depression. They do not do boring. They do not do dull.

This is the person to help you start that business. Full to the brim with energy and enthusiasm, they will be more excited than you about your new concept. Make the most of this time (and make a note of all their great ideas) because as soon as the door opens on the second day, Mars in Aries will be gone. It's not personal, it's just that the idea suddenly became dull for them.

Best job for a Mars in Aries? Obviously, a facilitator. A salesperson is just as good—all that movement from place to place and person to person. And who can resist that warm, friendly smile and that trusting nature? Aries does not do deception. They are what they appear. More than likely, someone will deceive *them* because they trust everyone with such an innocence it is almost sad to watch. Even so, Mars in Aries won't be destroyed by this. Their optimistic nature soon reasserts itself.

They are active and enthusiastic and cheerful people, but being ruled by the planet of war, Mars, they can also get angry and confrontational if they are thwarted in their aims. They don't like to be told no or that their plans are unrealistic. It's easy to bring that happy smile back, though. Just agree with them and let them get on with it. If they fall, they'll get up and try again. They need to make their own mistakes.

## *Mars in Taurus (Fixed Earth)*

Mars energy is well-contained in the practical sign of Taurus. It is purposeful and directed toward a positive objective. Mars in Taurus people are capable and consistent, setting themselves achievable goals. No amount of personal effort puts them off; no obstacles sidetrack them. Success may take a bit longer than they originally thought, but they always get there in the end. Patience is their best virtue.

When Mars is in Taurus, the need to build and to own (possess) is strong. It might be another person or it might be their own property and land, but once they have it, they hang on to it. If they lose what they believe to be theirs, they are usually devastated. It is a very personal thing, having devoted all their time and energy toward achieving their aim. They don't really get depressed, but they might grind to a halt for a while. Eventually, Mars in Taurus will rally themselves because they have to build something to feel content.

Both sexes are inclined toward faithfulness and loyalty. They seek a partner who also wants a secure foundation and they have immense patience and staying power, more than enough to ride the storms of life while making sure their loved ones are safe and secure.

Their worst fault is stubbornness. Mars in Taurus devotes all their energy to their own goals and don't have much energy leftover for fitting in with other people. If they are tired, nothing will drag them out on a walk with you. Like their symbol the bull, they are pretty immovable if they decide they don't want to do something. But they will still be there when you get back, and pretty much forever if they have their way.

They adore luxury and comfort and all the sensuous pleasures, so if they have great meals, pleasant surroundings, and a loved one to snuggle up with, they are pretty much in heaven. Their whole life's aim is to gain safety and security in everything, and once they have their own home and their own partner and are fully content with a sense of relaxed well-being, nothing on Earth will shift them. Mars in Taurus partners are stayers. Bear that in mind if you decide to take one on, you can't shake them off.

They choose jobs that are safe. It is harder nowadays to find a safe and secure occupation, but if there is one, Mars in Taurus will find it. Many of them like to use their hands and do physical labour. They are the strong, silent types, men and women both. They enjoy nature, so they may seek an outdoors occupation.

Both sexes are great cooks, and both have enormous patience and oodles of tolerance. They never get sidetracked and they never lose their way. They are calm, assured, steady, and trustworthy; employers take note. They may not be fast, but they are reliable with a capital R.

## Mars in Gemini (Mutable Air)

To get straight to the point, Mars in Gemini will have scattered energies. Mars is life force and drive. Gemini is the sign of the twins, so there are two people to please. One might like something, the other something else. Gemini will switch in the blink of an eye between the two, and each twin loves excitement, variety, and change.

It is quite obvious that Mars in Gemini people are not going to settle for a boring career. In fact, the word *settle* is not one they recognise. Why settle when the world is full of interesting possibilities? Geminis are whizz kids with the written and spoken word. They sparkle and talk, talk and sparkle, and can juggle fifty things at the same time.

Careers in media are almost a certainty. They love to be where something is happening with the people who make it happen. They adore celebrity culture; they know all the "in" places to go, all the gossip, and all the latest fashion trends right up to the minute. Mars in Gemini knows who is wearing whom and why. They love to travel and talk at the same time. Their element is the air and they love to fly.

Because their life force is so scattered—because they try to do so much and be all things to all people—to preferably be in more than one place at a time, they can only skim the surface of things. Time is needed for in-depth study, and Gemini does not have the inclination to dig deep. They pick up snippets of information and that is all they need; with that, they sound knowledgeable about just about everything.

There is a great deal of mental energy in this position of Mars. They make great salespeople, able to relate to everyone in a friendly way, to make light conversation and jokes. Mars in Gemini people recall names and details well, so they will remember to ask after partners, sick mothers, and pets. They can sell anything, even without believing in the product they are selling.

Geminis are the vital link that draw people together. They initiate conversations and make suggestions, and they always know the best person for a job, having any number of contacts for every occasion.

Just because they are flighty and find it hard to stick with one job or task for long does not mean they lack intelligence. On the contrary, they are very bright and alert and have retentive memories and sharp, witty humour. Think of a television talk show host or comedian and you have the image of a Gemini. Quick, witty, clever, yet it is all apparently achieved with complete ease.

Mars in Gemini people diffuse tense situations immediately with a quick word and a new idea. They lighten situations and make everything fun—but they may not stay around to see the difference they have made; they are off on new adventures.

## *Mars in Cancer (Cardinal Water)*

Mars reflects an individual's life force and drive. In the protective sign of Cancer, it will express itself in the desire to be caring to others, particularly through the career. These are the people who unstintingly help others in a myriad of ways, from being a good neighbour to organising charity fundraisers, from working in the health sector to saving lives as a doctor, nurse, or paramedic. You name it, if it has the end result of being beneficial to others, Mars in Cancer will be there. This is because their life has to have a deeper meaning than simply money in the bank. They don't want to pass through life without offering a helping hand to their fellow travellers.

On a personal level, their main aim is emotional security. Financial security is good as well, but Mars in Cancer can do without that more easily than they can an emotional bond, which is an essential for their well-being. Once they have that emotional bond, they are happier venturing out into the world knowing there is someone to turn to when things get tough. And by tough, we are not talking hard work—that's easy for them because they give of themselves all the time. No, it is what others *say* that bothers them most. Being so sensitive, they are easily hurt by what might be considered an innocuous remark. Cancer is the sign of the crab, after all. Inside that apparently tough exterior lurks a sensitive underbelly that is easily wounded.

Mars in Cancer really cannot forget an unkind remark or an attack on those they love. Thus, their drive is to protect themselves and their loved ones from harm. They are always understanding and sympathetic, but there is a fierce and protective anger ready to lash out at anyone who threatens their family.

If necessity forces them, Mars in Cancer is quite capable of having a demanding career. They are far more scared of not having material security than facing the world and its potential pains. Yet, they are only truly themselves when they return home and close the door on the world, safe and secure within the bosom of their family: those who really understand their vulnerability and sensitivity and who need them so much, and for whom they do so much.

## Mars in Leo (Fixed Fire)

There is something about Mars in Leo people that makes them noticeable. Perhaps it is the way they stand, very tall and straight, or the way their eyes glow with the joy of being alive. Or maybe it is their optimism and good humour? Whatever it is, there is no doubting their charisma and style. They exude dignity and grace.

Mars in Leo takes charge and organises, but they manage to do it in such a charming manner it is hard not to be beguiled by them. The fact is, they do not do menial tasks; those they delegate. They are best at telling others what to do, but no one really minds because Mars in Leo are not bossy, they're commanding. There is a difference, and it is not so subtle. No one likes being bossed around, but most of us recognise someone who is organised, efficient, capable, and commanding.

Make no mistake, these individuals are theatrical in all they do. They don't creep around quietly, nor do they work behind the scenes. They want a starring role, centre stage. Because of this, Mars in Leo people have the ability to take any situation and make a grand occasion of it.

When these people walk into a room, it is as if a light has been switched on. Suddenly there is fun and laughter and joy. Mars in Leo therefore creates the situation it needs most: love and admiration from friends and family. If they have a job that challenges their leadership qualities, even better.

It had to be said that they are not pussycats all the time. They are liable to roar, but only if their superior status is not recognised and acknowledged. Their anger, which is quickly aroused, fades just as fast, and they never bear a grudge or remember a dispute. Life is too short and too exciting to spoil it with anything as mundane as bad feelings.

Given the right atmosphere in which to live and work, individuals with this combination are at their very best. Hardworking, loyal, dignified, loving, kind, and protective—and not just of those they love, but of anyone who needs them.

## Mars in Virgo (Mutable Earth)

These are the people who voluntarily choose to do the jobs that most of us avoid. That's because they actually enjoy dotting the i's and crossing the t's. And let's face it, someone has to do it! Someone has to painstakingly plan the train and bus timetables, make sure the accounts are filed on time, and double-check that the restaurant food has been ordered. Someone has to make sure that meeting of global foreign ministers is planned to the finest detail. Ta-da! Mars in Virgo appears, cool as you like, organising, planning, and making sure everything is in place and running like clockwork.

Routine doesn't worry them. In fact, they like it. It makes them feel secure when they know where they have to be at a certain time each day. They are a little lost when routine is taken away, but it isn't long before they find umpteen other things to attend to. After all, the world is a disorganised place, so there is never a lack of work for those who like to sort things out and tidy up.

Mars in Virgo wants to be of use. They give a full day's work for a full day's pay, too, and they never shirk their responsibilities, so employers take note. Modest in the extreme, these are the people others hardly notice. They slip in and out of a room, quietly busy, actually managing to do a huge amount of work, unseen. Therefore, they do get taken for granted. It is only when they are off sick or on holiday that people notice their absence, and then it's probably because chaos sets in after a few days without them.

By the time people notice what a wonderful contribution Mars in Virgo made—both at work and in a marriage—they have often given up and moved on. Their sign is mutable, so if pushed really hard and taken for granted once too often, they will go. Being in the limelight is anathema to them, so they are not about to blow their own trumpet, but everyone likes to be appreciated and thanked now and then, and Mars in Virgo is no different.

## Mars in Libra (Cardinal Air)

When Mars is in Libra, there is a pressing need to keep the peace, to avoid people who upset them, to weave a path that causes as little disruption and unpleasantness as possible. Life can be a gritty affair and Libra isn't really a down-to-earth person—more so an angel from another realm. So, if they have an ambition (and they might, but it will be hard to keep their enthusiasm going), it will be to bring harmony to people and life. Mars in Libra seeks to teach others about compromise and peaceful cohabitation, to show them how to appreciate and understand another's point of view, to accept that we all have opinions and none is more valid than the other.

Their energy is of the mind, not the body. All effort is extended in working out solutions that bring a peaceful conclusion to events. Work-wise, then, they can be anything from lawyers to party planners. Having an eye for beauty and design, planning a party or media event (where real life is temporarily suspended and people pretend everything is wonderful) is something Mars in Libra excels at. Home design and decoration also interest them—as long as the budget is unlimited. They'd rather design a millionaire's house than a row of terraces, it has to be said. They can be fashion designers, too, but the clothes will be impossibly glamorous and expensive.

Best of all, though, is a place where Mars in Libra can put to use their excellent way with words. Marriage guidance is a good place to find them, as is a psychologist's couch. If they have aimed high, you will find them in foreign offices attempting to broker peace deals with warring factions or countries. Or they might be writers, working in their beautiful study with gentle music playing. The books? Fiction probably, especially romances where it is all about the chase and not the action between the sheets. They might enjoy penning a murder mystery because working out the convoluted motives appeals to their clever minds, but the murders will be glossed over: no unpleasant descriptions, and definitely secondary to the well-thought-out denouement at the end.

Their cardinal energy is directed into making life as pleasant as possible, so if a job or situation becomes unpleasant, they will leave. Being so fair-minded, they give people and places plenty of chances before they leave. But, it has to be said, what they would rather do is... nothing. That is what they do best. And no one does nothing the way Libra does: with style, beauty, elegance, and charm.

Marrying into money is probably high on the list of priorities for a Libra Mars. That way they can design the house (or houses) beautifully and dress to impress and just be the lovely, sweet, beautiful people they are.

## Mars in Scorpio (Fixed Water)

Planets in Scorpio become intense and emotional, so if fiery Mars is here, it's best not to lock horns with this person because Scorpio always wins. Once they have decided on a plan of action, nothing and no one will come between them and it. Scorpio is a fixed sign, and Mars in Scorpio is relentless in their pursuit of what they want; they leave no stone unturned and no avenue unexplored. The subject will be thoroughly examined from all angles, and they will squeeze every last drop from it. Hence, Mars in Scorpio people make incredibly good detectives or researchers. It doesn't matter what subject they choose; they will plumb it to its depths and then some. They do nothing lightly. Whatever they undertake, they give of themselves wholly.

Great, then, to have Mars in Scorpio on your side in business. They usually have very canny insights and clever new ideas to keep the money flowing in. Listen to them, give them the freedom to act independently, and *trust* them. They don't trust anyone, but be assured if a Mars in Scorpio says they'll do something, they will, by whatever means they have to.

They play their cards close to their chest because they cannot accept or admit defeat. Inside, a little bit of them dies when they lose. They really believe they are better than everyone else—and to be fair, they usually are—so to be proven wrong is a crushing blow. If they have to admit defeat, at least let them do it privately. Public humiliation is anathema to them, which is why they make sure they know all the facts before presenting them to anyone, let alone the world at large. They rarely let others know their thoughts until they have looked at every angle and sussed out possible problems without seeing a single loophole. By the time Mars in Scorpio shares their idea with someone else, it is likely to be as polished as possible, yet this is the first anyone else will know about it. They research and check and check again. No way will they present their idea until they are in a position where they can't be ridiculed or teased. They take everything in stride, apart from failure.

If Mars in Scorpio is successful, you won't find them shouting in the street or crowing about it. They will turn up for work as if nothing has changed, but do not for one minute believe they aren't affected. They just don't show it. Everything they undertake is pursued with deep inner persistence, immense drive, and tremendous seriousness, and they *must* win.

A word of warning: do not cross a Scorpio Mars. It may not be immediately evident that they are angry about something. They show nothing on their faces, and their mannerisms probably won't change. This is because they are quite capable of biding their time until the right moment, and then they will strike. Their symbol is the scorpion, remember? It may be such a long time before they get their revenge that everyone else will have forgotten the inciting incident, but Scorpio never forgets, and they always get even.

## Mars in Sagittarius (Mutable Fire)

Mars in Sagittarius people are nothing if not direct. They zoom straight to the heart of the matter, bounding along with the optimism of a child, seeking something—anything really, whatever it is that has just caught their imagination.

Travel is one such thing. They have a basic need for personal freedom, and there is so much in the world to explore and discover—all those countries, all those different cultures, religions, and ideas! They like ideas and are fascinated by what others think. It doesn't matter if it is the postman or an Indian guru, Sagittarius wants to know their minds, their thoughts, and their passions.

Mars is life force and drive. In the sign of Sagittarius, it gives a restless, seeking, searching quality that prevents this sign from ever being able to settle in one place, or even with one person. They need adventure and excitement; they need to have something to look forward to and plan.

They are also extremely blunt and honest. If people can't take the unvarnished truth, it's best they don't ask a personal question. Still, at least others know where they stand with them. People won't have to spend ages wondering what Mars in Sagittarius meant when they said something.

Other drawbacks? The inability to stick with one course of action. Starting something and not finishing it. Being easily distracted. Having too many irons in the fire, scattering their energy far and wide.

But hey, it's a small price to pay when you will have the most adventurous, exciting, enthusiastic person in the world as your friend/partner. They will never slow down; Mars in Sagittarius does not give in to getting old. They'll be off on their bike, hiking a long-distance path, or skydiving at the age of eighty. Who wants slippers by the fire, anyway?

### Mars in Capricorn (Cardinal Earth)

Brutal facts first? Mars in Capricorn people are not going to set the world on fire. They are not going to have an exciting job, leap from aeroplanes for a laugh, zip-line across a ravine, or bungee jump from a mountain. Nor will they be surfing, kiting, skating, or having a go at any other slightly risky hobby. They are a bit on the dull side, if truth be told. A bit boring, a bit old-fashioned. They have those slightly obscure jobs in the back of banks and financial institutions, managing other people's finances in ways unknown to most of us. They will be advisors to ancient institutions and the supporters of traditional societies.

Capricorns of both sexes aim high in life. They know from an early age where they want to be and will have worked out how to get there. You can find them in libraries, studiously researching, bent over ancient tomes with rapt attention. And if they're on the computer, it won't be social media they are looking at. Instead, they're studying up on facts and details relevant to their long-term life plan. They won't be counselors or psychologists, nor salespeople or advertising executives. Their job will be one that has been around for a long, long time: government, politics, finance, the New York Stock Exchange. And they aim to be the head of it, to be running the whole kit and caboodle.

No award or accolade is ever refused. Success is their *raison d'être*, so why would they refuse? Acknowledgment really means something to Mars in Capricorn, a gold star for all their efforts—and their efforts will be considerable. They will have earned whatever they receive in the way of money and status. While others were out partying and having sun-drenched holidays, they were working.

### Mars in Aquarius (Fixed Air)

The planet Mars represents drive and ambition. In the sign of Aquarius, the motivations are for the good of mankind. Hence, Mars in Aquarius will work in areas that can enhance the human condition, be it the medical field, information technology, or a charitable organisation. Of course, they are found everywhere, but somewhere in their remit will be the goal of improving our lot here on Earth.

This need to do good is impersonal. There is no need for inner salvation, no desire for fame and fortune. These are the last things on their minds, as is security. Mars in Aquarius lives and lets live. If they can assist their fellow humans along the way, they will gladly stretch out a helping hand, but they won't give of themselves wholly. The need for personal independence is too great.

There is a certain coolness and detachment about them. Their dreams are not of the romantic variety, nor are they emotional people. Friendship is important, as is a harmonious working environment, and they will be the last ones to stir up trouble. Mars in Aquarius doesn't do drama, nor are they bothered about who gets the accolades for a job well done. Because they have a nonexistent ego, they are more than willing to give advice, to help and assist in any way they can, and to generally be of use without any mention or thanks at all.

They enjoy being at the forefront of advances in areas like space, electronics, and research. They can handle large organisations and myriads of people with calm equanimity and will listen impartially to all views, and they can apply their logic and reasoning skills to all aspects of life.

Being innately shy, an Aquarius Mars will never push themselves forward, shout, or create a scene. They rarely lose their temper. In fact, they can be so reasonable at times it may drive others crazy! But when the chips are down and someone needs to work late or over the weekend, Mars in Aquarius will do it, and they won't expect extra pay, nor any thanks for doing it. Their partner will be used to being abandoned any hour of the day or night, so Aquarius won't even have to ring home.

In reality, they are better working alone at random hours when the spirit of genius overtakes them. Their intelligence is stirred by a vision of the future only they can see, and if an idea comes at three in the morning, they can happily start working on it then. They don't resonate with the same rhythms of life as the rest of us, but drift in some otherworldly sphere where time is a concept, not a reality.

When an Aquarius Mars unexpectedly heads for the door (which is likely), it will be when life suddenly feels like it is closing in on them. Smile and hold the door open for them. Don't worry, they will come back. Their sign is fixed, so they don't like change, just freedom.

### Mars in Pisces (Mutable Water)

All the more aggressive planets lose their oomph in Pisces. Mars is action and drive, full of reckless adventure and energy. Dunk it in water of Pisces and what happens? It fizzles out.

Mars in Pisces will not be aggressive or driven or very ambitious at all, and when the planet of ambition loses its direction, everything grinds to a halt. All of Mars's energy and enthusiasm gets dumped on by a cold wash. Is it any wonder, then, that these individuals cannot decide what to do with their lives or which career to follow? How can they decide when there are so many choices?

Even if they do finally choose something, they will never be very motivated. Worldly success is of no interest to them. However, they do understand the need to keep a roof over their head and food on the table, so they will get a job. But it won't be a high-profile career. More likely, it will be a behind-the-scenes occupation that doesn't ask too much of them. They don't have much stamina or staying power. And even when working, they will take regular breaks to rest; maybe sitting at their desk staring out the window at the birds or the trees or the sky, dreaming of being in other places.

They are understanding and sympathetic and take the burdens of others onto their own shoulders, so consequently, they get burnt out quickly. When that happens, they get irritable and snappy. Don't get annoyed with them. Instead, step back and allow them some space. They will find their own balance in due course.

Highly intuitive, probably psychic, Mars in Pisces would ideally prefer a job that involves helping others. The professions that attract them most are those with some connection to art, faith/religion, caretaking, counselling, or mystical subjects. If they are employed in some other field, they will choose one of these to do in their spare time.

If they happen to earn a lot of money along the way, it will be completely accidental—and knowing Mars in Pisces, they are just as likely to give it away to a family member in need.

# Jupiter
## ♃

**Affects:** Expansion, wisdom, higher learning, opportunity, abundance, luck, joy

Jupiter's position in a birth chart shows a person's lucky area. The qualities of the astrological sign it is in at birth describe where we experience the most joy and pleasure. Jupiter rules Sagittarius. Find the symbol for Jupiter in your chart. What sign is it in, and how do you think it will express itself in your life?

### Jupiter in Aries (Cardinal Fire)
The sign of Aries is all about expressing individuality. It is courageous and impetuous. Put the expansive planet Jupiter here and it will increase the lust for life.

These people will not be shrinking violets. Challenges will light their inner fire and new experiences will delight them; they never say no to new opportunities. They are their own best advertisement. They lead and others follow. A daredevil, larger than life, they are destined to blaze a trail through life.

### Jupiter in Taurus (Fixed Earth)
People with Jupiter here endeavour to surround themselves with the finer things in life, which will make them feel secure and comfortable. They will succeed in anything to do with land, property, real estate, gardening, building, or design. It's likely that money will come easily to them, though they might like a gamble now and then! They like the outdoors and see natural beauty in both landscapes and people.

## Jupiter in Gemini (Mutable Air)

Gemini is the sign of ideas and communication. This is their forte. Highly sociable and friendly, they delight in talking, writing, speaking, and passing on information. To get that information, they ask questions, listen to people, form ideas, use their minds, and formulate and assimilate. Therefore, a career in writing, acting, speaking, teaching, presenting, or even filmmaking will all provide stimulation and joy.

## Jupiter in Cancer (Cardinal Water)

Cancerians are the nurturers of the world, not only for their own families but for anyone in need. With Jupiter here, they seek to protect and love everyone who comes into their sphere. Being a water sign, they are sensitive to the needs of others, intuitively understanding when people need help and support and knowing just how to provide it. They will excel at social work, cooking, home design, and family history.

## Jupiter in Leo (Fixed Fire)

Leos are extroverts; they love to stand out from the crowd and shine. Leos are often great actors and speakers, capable of holding an audience in the palm of their hands. Jupiter here denotes a larger-than-life, over-the-top personality that is capable of leadership and inspiring others, and Jupiter in Leo has a great sense of fun and play. Any sort of acting is an ideal way to express this energy, but they are also artistic, talented, and great with children.

## Jupiter in Virgo (Mutable Earth)

Virgo is the sign of discipline, structure, rules, regulations, boundaries, and discrimination. Jupiter here provides the ability to bring order from chaos, to realign and restructure, to hone skills and create good working environments. They are also good at service, but they are better at serving behind the scenes—an unsung hero, in effect. These people can analyse, chart, plan, and execute schemes that bring help and succour to others. Good careers for a Virgo Jupiter are medicine, healing, public service, charity work, or office work.

## Jupiter in Libra (Cardinal Air)

Libra's symbol is the scales. Justice, balance, and peace will be the watchwords of someone with Jupiter here. They go out of their way to bring harmony to all situations, so they make great mediators. A love of colour makes them good interior decorators with an eye for beauty in their surroundings. Other than that, the law, social activism, fashion, entertainment, and public relations are all good outlets with Jupiter here.

## Jupiter in Scorpio (Fixed Water)

Scorpio is infused with a deep, passionate energy. Used correctly, it can be a force to be reckoned with. All the mysteries of the world will be easy for these people to see and understand. This intense energy can be directed into helping others understand the cycles of birth and death and the way transformation works in people's lives. Psychology, psychiatry, sexual counselling, metaphysics, detective work, and esoteric subjects are those that will inspire and interest them.

## Jupiter in Sagittarius (Mutable Fire)

These are the seekers of knowledge. They want to find answers to the big questions: the meaning of life and humanity's reason for being here. They understand faith and other far-reaching concepts with their spiritual questioning. Jupiter is in its natural place here, so this is considered a very lucky position. Good things will come their way, allowing them to expand their knowledge even more. Great careers are those connected with horses, gambling, travelling, exploring, language, competitive sports, or any career that requires extensive study in old subjects.

## Jupiter in Capricorn (Cardinal Earth)

Those with Jupiter here are resourceful, determined, reliable, and capable. They have integrity and a love of tradition. They desire to create something enduring, and they don't mind how long it might take to climb the career ladder. These are the leaders in business, finance, large organisations, or the government. Their high standards are a watchword; people know they can assign a job to a Jupiter in Capricorn and they will do it to the very best of their ability and then some. A great way to express this energy is through city planning or being a politician, financier, advisor, or barrister—any career path that has a long history and good future prospects.

### Jupiter in Aquarius (Fixed Air)

Aquarians cannot walk to any tune but their own. Their natural home is unknown territory. They step along pathways only they can see in an effort to shock people out of their complacency, and in doing so, they make discoveries way beyond their time. They thrive in groups but often work alone, and they are best suited for careers in science, engineering, computing, physics, or esoteric subjects. They can be an artist who shocks, a musician who shows a new way of expressing a piece of work, or even a Nobel Prize winner.

### Jupiter in Pisces (Mutable Water)

Pisces is the sponge of the zodiac, intuitively feeling and knowing everything. Compassionate, understanding, imaginative, and fully aware of a world that few people can comprehend, they should channel their gifts into healing, art therapy, drama, music, or helping vulnerable or disabled children. They should live and work near the sea, as they need quiet time to renew their strength. Their high idealism, when combined with more active planets, can make the world a better place.

## Planets in Astrological Signs

- Planets in Aries: Act quickly and assertively
- Planets in Taurus: Become stable and practical
- Planets in Gemini: Become unsettled and intellectual
- Planets in Cancer: Become emotional and protective
- Planets in Leo: Become bolder and more expressive
- Planets in Virgo: Become practical and analytical
- Planets in Libra: Are concerned with creating harmony
- Planets in Scorpio: Act emotionally and intensely

- Planets in Sagittarius: Become unstable and concerned with personal freedom
- Planets in Capricorn: Become pragmatic and cautious
- Planets in Aquarius: Become erratic, freer, and unpredictable
- Planets in Pisces: Become sensitive, receptive, and responsive

*Three*
# THE HOUSES

*L*ook closely at your chart and you will see short lines on the outside of the chart wheel itself. There will be twelve of these lines. Sometimes they are all black lines, but some charts show a few in red and the rest in black. These denote the houses.

Houses are areas of life. They are determined according to what time a person is born, hence the need for an accurate time of birth. The astrological sign rising on the eastern horizon at the time of birth is used to denote the ascendant, which is why it is often called the rising sign. The astrological sign here can be any of the twelve. This is considered the first house. The rest of the houses are numbered consecutively, anti-clockwise. Usually, there is a number beside each line denoting which house it is—except the start of the first house, the ascending house, when sometimes a short red line is used; often it also has the abbreviation AC.

Regardless of which astrological sign is in a house in your chart, it takes its general characteristics from the astrological sign that rules it. For example, the first house is ruled by Aries, the second by Taurus, the third by Gemini, and so forth. How this works will become clearer as you work through the information below.

It might be a good idea to take notes about your own chart as you work through this chapter so that by the end, you will have a clear understanding of how each of your twelve houses work in your own life.

## First House (The Ascendant/Rising Sign)

The first house is all about how we want the world to see us. It's our point of contact with strangers, the characteristics we present to people when they meet us for the first time. It is the mask we wear to protect our inner, vulnerable self. There is not always a planet in the first house, but the astrological sign is still used as a mask. This is unique, as usually we are not drawn to houses (areas of life) that do not have a planet.

What is the sign of your ascendant? You should be able to recognise the symbols of the astrological signs by now. It is likely to be a completely different sign than the one your sun occupies (although not always).

No matter what your sun sign is, you will show the characteristics of your ascending sign to others, but it won't be the real you—it is only a facade you use as protection. Later, if you get to know someone better, you will allow them to see more of the real you. You won't adopt your ascendant's characteristics as part of your personality, but you will be comfortable displaying them as your outward persona.

If there is a planet in the first house, you might feel it will complicate matters when it comes to interpretation. Not really. Just assess how that planet in that astrological sign works, and then the rest is easy; that is what you will let others see first.

For example, someone with the moon in the first house will show themselves to be empathic and caring and will appear receptive to others. Mercury in the first house will show itself in someone very talkative, Venus will come across as attractive and charming, Mars might be someone who always argues or forces their opinion on others, and Jupiter will be a larger-than-life person full of generosity and grand ideas.

What if someone has the sun in their first house? This means that what you see is what you get. There is no hiding behind the ascendant because there is nowhere to hide. The sun must express itself because it is who we are. People with their sun in the first house are often overpowering because we are hit by their personality as soon as we meet them—there is no gradual opening and revealing.

We looked at the astrological signs in chapter 1, but here is a brief recap. And remember, you won't become your ascendant, but you naturally show these characteristics to others when you first meet them.

## Aries Ascendant

You come across as impulsive, friendly, talkative, and outgoing. You like to appear confident and capable and often dress as a tomboy, or at least prefer a sporty look. People see you as energetic, cheerful, and up for adventures and challenges. You aren't subtle, and you don't mind others being aware of an impetuous, bossy side; you are quite proud of this tough persona that stands its ground. Sometimes you can come across as hardheaded, impatient, and argumentative. You stand up for what you think is right, and you have no problem voicing your opinions.

## Taurus Ascendant

People see you as dependable, reliable, and totally trustworthy. You present yourself as patient, slow to change, slow to anger, and stubborn, sometimes implacably so. You dislike anything new, anything different, and anything unsettling. You enjoy routine and are unlikely to want adventures. Outwardly, you present as someone who is not introspective or intuitive, and your love of comfort and luxury means you prefer your own fireside. You have earthy appetites, with a love of food and drink and an inability to deny yourself sensual pleasures. Money and belongings are important. You don't say much, but you like to help others in practical ways.

## Gemini Ascendant

Your outer persona is that of a changeable and restless person who is flexible and adaptable. You are glib and a good conversationalist, and you know just how to lighten an atmosphere. Your symbol is the twins, so you have two sides to your personality and can effortlessly switch between each. Hard to pin down, you often make arrangements and then cancel them when something else comes along. So you're not very reliable, but you are friendly and light and fun. You cannot cope with people who are emotional, dramatic, or dependent, and you will make a quick exit. You like being fashionable and are keen to know the latest gossip.

## Cancer Ascendant

Cancer ascendants like to be seen as sympathetic and emotional. You are happy to show your protective, compassionate, empathic side to others, and you encourage them to open up to you about their problems. Tears come to your eyes very easily, and you are sentimental about the past, which you view through rose-coloured spectacles. If someone lets you down, you find it hard to forgive and even harder to forget. You enjoy making people feel looked after and like home-making and caring for others. You think that showing emotional support to others is important, and you like nothing better than long talks about your (and their) emotions.

## Leo Ascendant

Your symbol is the lion, which accurately describes the innate dignity and pride you portray to others. You enjoy being praised and require respect. Your need for admiration means you seek a position of authority, and you never feel entirely happy in a lowly situation. Vain, generous, and affectionate, yes, but you can roar like the lion if annoyed. With family and friends, you are warm, loving, and protective. You are enthusiastic about most adventures and have a childlike love of life. Both men and women dress to impress and like to be noticed when they enter a room.

## Virgo Ascendant

Practical, service-minded, and dutiful, you enjoy attention to detail and have great organisational skills. Virgos work best behind the scenes, out of the limelight, doing what they do best: tidying up the messes the rest of us leave behind. You can turn your hand to anything that involves details, and your concentration is phenomenal. You will serve selflessly without expecting praise; you do things because you are kind and hardworking. Being so able to see faults and failings makes you critical of others, so beware of becoming a fussy nagger. But that's your worst fault, and it's only because you can't abide untidiness in a person or a place.

## Libra Ascendant

You like to appear sensible, reasonable, logical, and balanced. The symbol of Libra is the scales, so you endeavour to be calm and harmonious in your emotions and judgments. You come across as eminently reasonable, though you are unlikely to take sides in an argument. Ruled by Venus, most Libras are attractive, and you will always put your best foot forward and dress well. You rarely lose your temper and never raise your voice, and you are always unfailingly polite, but you are inclined to bouts of laziness when the scales are out of balance.

## Scorpio Ascendant

Scorpio ascendant is an enigma because Scorpio is secretive, so even when this sign is used as a mask, it hides its true feelings and intentions. You enjoy being hard to fathom and tend to watch and wait when you meet people so you can suss out their motives and what they want from you. Thus, you tend to be cautious about allowing people to get to know you well. Even those you've known a long time will never know everything about you, as you always keep something of yourself back. However, you are not to be messed with. If people let you down or betray you, your anger is cold and implacable. You never forgive, and you certainly never forget.

## Sagittarius Ascendant

Sagittarius ascendants are incredibly friendly and always up for fun and adventure. You like nothing more than being busy with a new project or idea, and because you love people, you have numerous friends and plans to meet up. Your door is always open. You are genuine and honest with people—probably too honest, if truth be told, because you are the most blunt and truthful of all the signs. If people ask a question, you always give a direct answer and can inadvertently tread on sensitive people's toes. Your restless movement is due to your interest in absolutely everything. You enjoy travelling, intellectual discussions, exploring, foreign languages and cultures, esoteric subjects, religious beliefs, and learning.

### Capricorn Ascendant

You come across as modest, cautious, and reserved, maybe even a little shy, but there is something reliable and trustworthy about you. People know you won't mess around and play games. No matter what age you are, there is a capability in your manner. Others know they can ask you advice, and you will always respond wisely. You have no interest in a false facade—you are who you are—but you don't suffer fools at all. And while you are happy to offer assistance and advice to those in need, you won't give the time of day to people who won't make good use of it; you reserve your considerable wisdom for those you consider worthy of receiving it. You are hardworking and traditional and have lasting values. You like the best in life, but you can be incredibly abstemious with yourself.

### Aquarius Ascendant

Friendship is the Aquarian keyword, so you are easygoing and accepting of people from all walks of life. You make no moral judgments and have all types of people on your long list of friends. You listen with fascination to what people feel and think and enjoy observing them because you find life and people intensely curious. You love discovering new things—the more unusual the better—and because of your innate need to shock, you are liable to do or say outrageous things just for the fun of it. You are independent and prefer to do things alone. Unwilling and unable to toe the line, you enjoy being original and unpredictable. You live life in your own way and will not be tied down. Fun and friendly, you will head for the exit if things get too stressful or emotional.

### Pisces Ascendant

You present yourself to others as sensitive, dreamy, and compassionate. You are incredibly understanding and sympathetic, and people sense this and often turn to you for help when life has been unkind or when disaster strikes. You always try and help but your stamina is limited, and while you empathise and verbally support those in need, you instinctively know when to step back for your own well-being. In fact, even though you are naturally understanding, you are actually quite cool and detached because of this vulnerability. You know when enough is enough. You always take the path of least resistance and avoid situations that are stressful, so you are not terribly reliable despite your sweet nature. You appear vague and muddleheaded, but you are often psychic.

## Second House (Money, Possessions, Security)

The second house is ruled by Taurus, the second astrological sign. Therefore, it is concerned with possessions, material security, financial matters, and whom and what we own—*whom* because, whether we like it or not, some people see others as belonging to them.

The astrological sign in the second house shows how an individual will view finances, security, and money. Look at your own chart. What astrological sign is the second house? How do you think this affects how you feel about money and possessions?

The sign of Aries in the second house will make people impulsive with money and inclined to take risks. Taurus is perfect here because it is its own sign; it will build and accumulate money and possessions. Gemini will make money using words and communication, maybe as a teacher or lecturer or writer, perhaps as a salesperson. Cancer will save money for a rainy day and work hard to build financial security for themselves and their loved ones. Leo will spend, spend, spend in an effort to live the high life. Virgo will enjoy keeping a detailed financial record of their spending. Libra likes balance, so will take a measured, sensible view of money. With that said, they like the finer things in life, so they will spend their money making sure everything is as comfortable and luxurious as possible. Scorpio will be secretive and canny with money and property. Sagittarius will take risks and have too many financial irons in the fire. Capricorn will be extremely cautious with their money and possessions, building slowly until they feel secure. Aquarius will act unpredictably in money matters. Pisces will be muddled and easily misled.

Any planet in the second house will be used in financial matters. The moon may hoard money for a rainy day and feel a sense of emotional security from their possessions. Mercury will use words and communication to make financial gains. Venus will use charm to get what they want or choose careers that are concerned with beauty or design. Mars is driven to make money and security. Jupiter will gamble and take risks.

The sun in the second house means the person will get their sense of identity from what they own. Many millionaires (or certainly very rich people) have the sun in the second house.

## Third House (Communication, Siblings, Neighbours)

This house, like the sign of Gemini that rules it, is all about communication. The astrological sign here describes how we speak, what we say, and whether we like to teach or write or learn. It also hints at whether we are quiet, chatty, reticent, or outgoing. The sign of the third house shows how we relate to others and rules our attitudes and feelings about our siblings, neighbours, and close community.

The astrological sign shows how we feel about this house. Aries will actively take part in the community. Taurus will be someone slow to speak and talk. Gemini will be happy here, as this is its own house. Cancer will express its caring side verbally and in the community. Leo will want to be actively involved in community affairs, preferably in charge of them. Virgo will look after people close to them and maybe keep the accounts for local groups. Libra's words will be reasoned and they will resolve disputes in their community. Scorpio will be enigmatic with siblings and neighbours, so it will difficult to really get to know them. Sagittarius will flit from subject to subject. Capricorn will have an interest in history and may research and write about the past. Aquarius will want to shock with their words and will be erratic with siblings and friends. Pisces will be imaginative in their thoughts and speech—and forgetful, too!

A planet in this house draws us to that area. For example, the sun in the third house means you get your sense of identity from this house, so regardless of what sign it is in, the sun will express itself through language, teaching, and writing. Sun in Gemini in the third house indicates a teacher; this is so accurate it is uncanny. Those with sun in Scorpio in the third house are often university lecturers or have studied a subject in-depth and want to pass on information. The moon in the third house will express emotions through speech and writing. Venus will have a love of writing and studying. Mars might produce someone aggressive and confident in their speech who is a fully active member in community affairs. Jupiter in the third house indicates a love of words and feeling good in the community.

# Fourth House (Home and Family)

The fourth house is at the bottom of a birth chart. Like a tree, this is the secure foundation we rise from, so planets in the fourth house want to maintain security within the family and will use their energy to secure these foundations. IC is short for *Imum Coeli*, which means "the bottom of the sky." Although it is a very old term, the abbreviated form of IC is still used today to denote the fourth house.

The fourth house, on a mundane level, is the type of physical house we seek. Look at the astrological sign here. Now that you understand how the signs work, see if you can assess your own fourth house sign. Aries will want a clean, airy, and functional house. Taurus will adore its home and seek to fill it with possessions. Gemini will want a modern house filled with the latest technology. Cancer rules the fourth house, so they put all their effort into looking after their family and making their home a haven of comfort and security. Leo will want a grand house. Virgo will look after their family and home, and it will be spotless. Libra will create a haven of peace from the outside world. Scorpio will be ultra-protective of their family and home. Sagittarius will seek a home that is large and grand because it's ruled by expansive Jupiter. Capricorn is able to sleep on bare boards, so their home will be functional. Aquarius's home will be unique in some way. Pisces will live amidst chaos.

On a deeper level, the fourth house describes the family we came from and therefore the type of family we try to create when we are older and independent. We model not only our parents' behaviour but the way we were brought up and how we lived. Thus, the fourth house is what we came from and what we try to obtain.

For example, someone with the sign of Sagittarius in the fourth house will probably have had many homes while growing up, forever on the move. Thus, when grown up, they will also move frequently, but it will be an upwardly mobile quest, always bigger and better because Jupiter is the ruler of Sagittarius.

Aquarius in the fourth house come from an unusual background and may recreate that by wanting something different, unusual, or even outrageous! They may try to live in a way that is out of the norm.

Libra in the fourth house thinks of their home as a haven of peace and harmony; their own background will have been pleasant, likely with an emphasis on the arts or music or design, and this is how they want to live their own life.

We interpret planets in exactly the same way, but apply them to this particular house. Planets in the fourth house will be used to find and create a home/family/community, but they will also have been evident in a person's upbringing.

When the sun is in the fourth house, people will get their sense of identity from their home and family, and they might choose to work from home in later life.

## Fifth House (Self-Expression, Artistic Endeavours, Love Affairs, Children)

Like all of the houses, this covers more than one aspect of life, but all aspects of the fifth house are related to self-expression. It's about showing our talents to others, relating to others, being ourselves, enjoying ourselves; basically, our love of life and how we express that.

This house is ruled by the sign of Leo, which is ruled by the sun, so it's easy to see why self-expression is the buzzword for this house. To that end, this is the house of actors and artists, people who use either themselves or a medium like art or music as a way of expressing their unique style and personality.

Above and beyond this, the fifth house also shows our views to love affairs. The fifth house is concerned with enjoyment, and being in love is certainly a joyous time in life. The sign and any planets here reveal our attitude to having fun generally—do we like a social life, are we happy to party the night away, or do we prefer cosy nights in? Our desire for children is shown here, too. When we take our kids out for the day, we are engaging in a fifth house activity.

The fifth house is a touchy-feely place. We want direct physical contact, so as strange as it may seem, this is also the home of the medical profession. This is because doctors and health workers have to touch strangers, sometimes intimately, in order to help them. However, before this judgment can be made, there have to be distinct caring aspects in the chart (specifically, planets in Cancer or the sixth house).

The astrological sign of the fifth house will show how it is viewed. Aries will be all cheerful bonhomie when at social events, full of enthusiasm. Taurus will want to make money from fifth house matters. Gemini will enjoy talking about these aspects and gossiping with others. Cancer will be caring to others in some way that reflects the aspects of this house. Leo will enjoy everything about the fifth house and will strive to be the centre of attention, dancing on tables, singing karaoke, or pursuing a career that brings them in close contact with others and leads to admiration or praise—more aptly, becoming an actor. Virgo will find the fifth house all too seedy and distasteful and will try to get people to clean up their acts. Libra will resolve disputes, especially those that involve affairs, children, or artistic expression. Scorpio can go either way—delving deep into the seedier side of life or trying to encourage people to take a higher path. Sagittarius is likely to study and philosophise about fifth house matters. Capricorn will find a career in one of these aspects. Aquarius will be intrigued and just observe. Pisces will be compassionate and understanding of people from all walks of life, probably artistic in some form.

To assess how any planet here works, think of it as having a Leo feel with a larger-than-life need to express itself. The moon will seek to be nurtured by praise and admiration and will feel comforted when surrounded by an admiring group of friends or colleagues. Mercury will like to talk, lecture, discuss, and counsel about fifth house issues and will be happy to show their verbal and mental skills to the world; writers often have this placement. Venus will adore being involved with everyone and will want to express itself in artistic endeavours and love affairs. Mars is driven to express itself here, so art, acting, or the medical professions are areas of life focus. Jupiter might go a bit over the top in this house, as it is already a look-at-me place; they will want to be in the spotlight and will revel in being admired.

The sun in the fifth house shows that the individual gets their sense of identity from this area. They will love being in charge and on display; this person requires admiration and praise for what they do.

## Sixth House (Work, Service, Health)

This house is viewed as the work house. Unlike the tenth, which is the career house, this is the place you literally roll up your sleeves and do physical work. Thus, planets here show an individual is happy to get their hands dirty.

For that reason, it is also known as the house of service. It is Virgo's house, the sixth, and Virgo is nothing if not dutiful, cleaning up and sorting out other people's messes. Because it is such a physical, hands-on house, it usually shows how an individual views their health, too, because keeping healthy requires a certain amount of self-discipline in eating and exercising habits, and all of this is displayed by Virgo and the sixth house.

The astrological sign here shows how we feel about our own health and how much interest we have in helping others in practical ways. Aries will take up sports. Taurus will probably work as a chef. Gemini will talk about health and fitness. Cancer is likely to be a nurse, paramedic, or someone who cares for others in the community in some way. Leo will be a personal trainer, a physiotherapist, or similar. This is Virgo's house, so they are happy to serve others in any way they can. Libra will design community buildings or work for a charitable organisation that provides advice on legal affairs. Scorpio might research fitness methods. Sagittarius will flit from job to job. Capricorn will be the money behind local projects and maybe own a fitness club. Aquarius might do humanitarian work. Pisces will be a charity worker or similar.

A planet wants to be actively used in this area. Someone with the sun here gets their sense of identity from serving others. They will quietly work behind the scenes because this house is not showy. They do the physical work demanded of those in need—hands-on caring and serving. They derive a great sense of fulfilment from this. They might have busy lives, but they will always find time to help others in practical ways and are the first to take on the role of carer despite their other commitments. It is worth noting that *any* planet in the sixth wants to help, but because the sun is where a person gets their sense of identity, there is a stronger, more compelling desire to serve.

It is impossible to be precise about how each planet will work because birth charts are so complex and varied, but if we use a literal interpretation, this is a rough idea: The moon gets an emotional kick from helping others or keeping fit. Mercury wants to talk or teach in this area. Venus will work in beauty, perhaps as a hairdresser or interior design, and offer these services to those who need care. Mars will be driven to keep fit and will work hard at their job. Jupiter will have never-ending love for those who need care and a special desire to help others.

## Seventh House (Marriage and Partnerships)

At the opposite side of the chart from the ascendant (AC) is the descendant (DC). The ascendant is how we show ourselves to the world, but the descendant and any planets in this house are used solely with other people, to attract and keep them.

The seventh house shows how we feel about marriage and long-term relationships (love affairs come under the fifth house), so the astrological sign here shows what type of partner we seek. It's quite clear. If the seventh house is in Aries, we like a fiery, active person. Taurus, someone earthy and reliable. Cancer, someone caring. And so on. We might literally choose that astrological sign as a partner or be drawn to them in general.

Any planet in the seventh house is used to attract a mate. If it's the moon, it will express itself by being empathic and understanding of the partner. Mercury here means that conversation is necessary in a relationship, and this person will have some clever, witty, and amusing chat-up lines. Women with Venus in the seventh house hardly have to do a thing; partners will be drawn to them like bees to a honey pot! The same goes for Mars in the seventh house in a man's chart.

As an example, imagine the astrological sign of Taurus in the seventh house. Let's put a planet in Taurus, say, Jupiter. This person wants someone Taurean; earthy, stable, secure. They're not attracted to a flighty person. But Jupiter means wining and dining, enjoying the luxuries of life, being a romantic in a larger-than-life way. Put that together and we can assume that this individual will look for someone rich. Wealth brings security. The partners that come into their life must be able to supply endless luxuries in order to feed the Taurean need for comfort, food, and security and Jupiter's larger-than-life appetite.

If the sun is in the seventh house, this is someone who gets their sense of identity from their partner. If there are no planets in the seventh house, it means you are not drawn to this area in particular, but when it comes to choosing a partner, you will still look for someone with the characteristics of the astrological sign in the seventh house. This is obviously not a conscious decision for people who don't understand astrology, but nevertheless, it's uncanny how many people choose their DC astrological sign in a partner.

You see how this works? Which astrological sign is the seventh house in your chart? You can see the type of partner you seek at a glance. Even if you are not drawn to exactly the same sign, it might be the same element. Are you drawn to fire, earth, air, or water signs? Is there a planet in your seventh house?

Note: People who marry for security rather than love often choose a partner who is the astrological sign in their fourth house.

## Eighth House (Sexuality, Psychology, Other People's Money, Death and Inheritance)

This house shows what we expect from others in financial terms. It also shows if we want to control or manipulate others through sexual, psychological, or financial means or if we want to help them by being a financial advisor, counselor, or academic in these areas. This house is traditionally ruled by Scorpio, so motives are often hidden.

How we feel about this house will depend on the astrological sign here. If it is a fire sign, there will be an open and direct approach to these matters. An earth sign will expect some financial remuneration from others, and air signs might want to counsel or discuss these matters. A water sign will be compassionate and caring. But a sign like Scorpio might not be quite so straightforward to analyse. They will be incredible psychologists and detectives, but as Scorpio always hides its motives, they may be tempted to use their abilities to control others via these means. The whole chart needs to be analysed before making any decision about this.

Someone with the sun in the eighth house might choose to be a psychiatrist or psychologist, a sexual counselor, or even a financial advisor. Moons in this house are incredibly sensitive and secretive and may seek to be emotionally involved in other people's psychological or financial issues. Mercury will find the areas the house covers of deep intellectual interest and may seek to solve mysteries; they will enjoy discussing the aspects of this house. Venus is imbued with a Scorpio-like passion to share their innermost feelings, insecurities, and desires. Mars will act like a Mars in Scorpio, driven and determined to find out secrets and hidden motives, so could be detectives or psychiatrists. Jupiter here makes a person intuitive in psychological matters and interested in other people's resources. Jupiter also provides protection against negative influences, so a Jupiter in the eighth house person cannot be influenced by others to go against their moral compass. Often, it means they will be taken care of by others.

## Ninth House (Travel, Higher Learning, Philosophies)

This is Sagittarius's house and deals with issues of travel, other cultures, higher learning, esoteric subjects (astrology being one), and being in the public eye. Because it is opposite the third house of communication and community, it indicates a step up in ambition and learning: study taken to a higher level, like university and beyond. It is where we develop our own theories and philosophies about life.

Houses that are in the top half of the chart like to be seen. We call it being in the public eye. People with a strong emphasis here are often happy to be in the limelight. Passing on what they know often involves either teaching in a higher education institution and/or writing and speaking. Many people with strong ninth houses (one or more of the personal planets here) are on television, which is the modern equivalent of teaching. Historians, travel programmes, and even wildlife documentaries are all embodiments of the ninth house because they aim to teach and educate and often involve travel to other countries to show foreign cultures.

The astrological sign of the ninth house shows our general feeling about this area of life, and a planet here will denote an interest in one or more of these areas. The sun shows the individual gets their sense of identity here and wants to become an expert in their field.

To recall the meaning of this house, think of an image of a university professor in their study. The third house involves activity within the community, but here it is private, individual study and the need to explore a subject in-depth. Some people seek to pass this on and some don't, but all planets here will be used in learning/teaching in some form or another. The moon will mean an emotional attachment to a subject the person loves. Mercury will be a communicator in their chosen field—an inspirational speaker, perhaps. Venus will indicate a love of old or esoteric subjects. Mars will lead to a drive to explain in-depth subjects and a fearless attitude toward them. Jupiter indicates searching for a bigger, deeper, more expansive meaning to life.

# Tenth House (Career)

The tenth house is also known as the midheaven (abbreviated MC). This house, being right at the top of the chart, is the pinnacle of worldly achievement and is called the career house. Planets here are used to achieve success through effort in the commercial/business world. To see what people want from their career, we look at the tenth house's astrological sign and any planets.

The same rules apply to this house as all the rest; a planet will draw us to this house. Having no planets in this house will create a feeling of disinterest in having a high-profile career. That is not to say the individual will not want to work, just that they have no inclination to strive for the highest accolades, to reach the pinnacle of their profession; maybe they are content to work at an ordinary job and then switch off when they get home.

The astrological sign alone provides information about how a person views a career and the type of job they might aspire to. A fire sign will want an active life, earth signs will seek a secure job with good financial remuneration, air signs will want a career that uses their logical and verbal skills, and water signs will seek something caring or artistic.

Planets here will express themselves in the career. The sun in the tenth house indicates someone who gets their sense of identity from their career. The moon will want a job that is caring. Mercury will use their verbal skills professionally. Venus may work in the areas of design, beauty, or fashion. Mars will be driven to succeed in their career. Jupiter will want a job with perks—meals out, a glamorous car, plenty of money to woo clients with.

For each and every interpretation, astrologers take the basic information about the signs and planets and apply it accordingly. Look at your own chart and think about how the astrological sign and any planets in the tenth house have influenced your choice of career. If you are unhappy in your job, perhaps this new information can assist you in finding a job more suited to your talents and abilities.

# Eleventh House (Friendships Based on Shared Values)

This house is ruled by Aquarius and deals with friendships with groups of like-minded people. These are not family members or ordinary friends, but rather joining with others who share the same values and ideals, perhaps by sitting on committees and/or being members of organisations. Aquarius is viewed as a humanitarian sign, but although some people do join groups that have altruistic aims, having a planet here does not necessarily mean this is a priority. Generally, people with planets here will happily join groups with whom they have interests in common, and if they can do some good, all the better.

However, those with the sun in the eleventh house will actively seek to change the world for the better, very much like an Aquarian would: by rocking the boat and not being afraid to speak out about perceived injustices.

People with an emphasis in this house are generally intelligent or a leader in their field. They are often invited to join select groups. These groups could be in any area or endeavour: artistic, scientific, medical, etc. Very often, these people end up making decisions on behalf of others, which is a better expression of this house's energy and direction.

Running through the planets here, the moon ensures an emotional attachment to the group, and often a caring cause is taken up. Mercury will be someone who wants to speak or preach about their chosen subject. Venus will advise on beauty, fashion, art, and design (or similar matters). Mars will be driven to force their views and opinions on the world. Jupiter will enjoy the ambience of a club-like atmosphere and the social side will be the draw, but there will also be a love of their fellow man and a real drive to make changes.

# Twelfth House (Spiritual Beliefs)

This house is the furthest away from the outside world. It is the innermost part of ourselves. It covers our spiritual beliefs (or otherwise), our secret self. Planets here are kept solely for our own private use.

The astrological sign in the twelfth house describes our feelings about religion and spiritual matters. Fire signs will feel driven to pursue a belief, earth signs will follow a traditional path in these matters, air signs will enjoy discussing them, and water signs will have an empathy with all mankind.

It is tempting to put vicars and priests in this house (and anyone involved in any religion will certainly have a strong planet here), but they stand up in the public eye to preach and thus have a desire to maintain a strong connection with others. Preaching one's own beliefs to others is not really a twelfth house activity, which is more of a place for quiet, private reflection.

A planet here will not be expressed outwardly, but the individual will feel it strongly. Those with the sun in the twelfth house are reclusive. Although they might appear to function in the world in a normal way by having a job and friends, in reality they are just putting on a front. They enjoy being alone to think. Some might actually retreat from the world.

Twelfth house people feel the need to go off on their own to quietly contemplate and meditate on the meaning of their existence. They view the commercial world and all the jostling for position and security as meaningless.

People with the moon in the twelfth house will not be able to emotionally relate to others in a way beyond friendship. They may have relationships, but they will stop short at making a full commitment because their emotional energy is not available to others. Very often, children with the moon in the twelfth house spend a lot of time alone in their rooms, but quite happily. They like their own company.

## Intercepted Houses

You can see from your own chart that unlike the astrological signs, which are all thirty degrees, not all houses are the same size. Sometimes there is more than one astrological sign within a house; occasionally there might be two or three astrological signs in a large house. The most important sign is the one with planets in it because planets draw the individual to the house they occupy. This is worth repeating, as it is so important.

If there are a few planets in a few signs all in one house, that just means the person will be adaptable in that area of life and can experience, at different times, all of the energies described by the planets and signs that are in that area of life.

However, some astrological signs have no house cusp; there is no small line coming from the sign to denote the start of a new house. These astrological signs are called *intercepted*. A planet in an astrological sign that has no house cusp has no way of accessing the area of life in which it is situated, so it cannot express itself in the outer world. This causes confusion in the individual. *Why don't people understand me?* they wonder. Without a house cusp from an astrological sign, the world does not see or feel any planet in that sign even though the individual can feel it.

The amount of distress it causes depends on the planet and the house. One student of mine had an intercepted moon in Scorpio in the fourth house, and no one understood her passionate emotions regarding her family and home; they stared at her blankly when she showed this part of herself. They did not see or feel her moon in Scorpio as it had no access to the outer world, so they ignored it, which was very frustrating for her. Once she understood why this happened, it was easier for her to accept when people misunderstood her.

## Motivation and Element Count in the Houses

Do you remember when, in chapter 1, you were asked to find out how many of the planets in your chart were fire, earth, air, and water, and then cardinal, fixed, and mutable? You came up with an astrological sign whose characteristics you inherited at birth.

To find out what the universe wants (which may not be the same), do the count again using the houses rather than the astrological signs. Start at the first house and count that as fire. The second would be earth, the third air, the fourth water, the fifth back to fire, the sixth earth, and so on. Count how many planet symbols are in each.

Now do the same again, but starting with the first house as cardinal, the second as fixed, the third mutable, the fourth cardinal again, and so on for the rest of the twelve houses.

Put them together. What astrological sign did you come up with? This shows what the world wants from you. Sometimes it is a very different sign than the one you inherited. Have a think about how this plays out in your life.

## Age Point

While we are looking at houses, it is important to mention age point. The astrological chart is like a clock. Think of the line denoting the start of the ascendant as the start of that clock. Work around the chart anti-clockwise (in other words, in the same direction the houses and signs go).

Regardless how small or large each house, it covers six years of someone's life. Thus, the first house starts at birth through six years old, the second house covers ages six to twelve, the third house covers ages twelve to eighteen, the fourth house covers ages eighteen to twenty-four, the fifth house covers ages twenty-four to thirty, and the sixth house covers ages thirty to thirty-six.

You can see that until the age of thirty-six, a person will be passing, by age point, through the bottom six houses of the chart. If we take into account the meaning of each house, it's easier to understand this idea.

The moment we are born, our ascendant is set. So, that is where we start. For the first six years of life we are passing, by age point, through the first house, so we express the qualities of the sign in the first house. We are children demanding our needs are met (reflected by the ruler of the first house being Aries). We go through the second house at ages six through twelve, and it is during this time we seek nurturing and security (second house ruled by Taurus). From the ages of twelve to eighteen, we delve into education more fully and start to express ourselves as an individual (third/Gemini). From ages eighteen to twenty-four, it is common to want to set up our own home (fourth/Cancer). From twenty-four to thirty, we learn more fully how to express ourselves in our own way; we may have children, too (fifth/Leo). By the time we pass through the sixth house from thirty to thirty-six, we are actively serving others (Virgo), usually because we have taken on responsibilities and have to buckle down and attend to them. During those years, we are also learning to become part of the community and what our place is in the world.

## Ages Thirty-Six to Seventy-Two

After thirty-six, continue to count every house as six years. Now we move toward the top of the chart. As we pass through each house, we are drawn to think about those aspects of life. Any planet we pass will be more fully activated.

The seventh house (ages thirty-six to forty-two) concerns our chosen relationships and how we relate to others. By this stage, generally, we are endeavouring to adjust our feelings and thoughts on how to handle our life partner so we can live harmoniously. If a partnership isn't working, this is when it becomes obvious. Perhaps another search is begun now that we know ourselves and better understand what we want in a partner.

The midheaven (tenth/Capricorn) is reached at age fifty-four, and often we are at the top of our career at this stage. We continue through the tenth house until we are sixty. We are then asked to join with others of like mind and ability in the eleventh house (Aquarius, ages sixty to sixty-six) and after that, we start to consider our own mortality and the meaning of our entire life as we pass through the twelfth house (ruled by Pisces, ages sixty-six to seventy-two).

After age seventy-two, we might retire from active life. Some become dependent on others again—the second childhood, as it is called. We might soon need help with the basics of life. Certainly, as we age, we will need help from friends, family, and the community to see us through the physical restraints of old age, so we come full circle into the bottom of the chart again.

Using the age point, you can see where you are at any given time in your life. The astrological sign you are passing through influences how you feel/act. If you are currently in an age point that is a fire sign, you might be more proactive. In earth, you are keener to establish security and hold on to what you have. In air, you are driven to research, learn, and read. In water, you are more sensitive to your own needs and those of others. Are you activating a planet's energy? You now know how the planets work, so that aspect of yourself will be triggered when you pass by.

Sometimes there is a vast gap in a chart where there are no planets. This will create a feeling of have stepped into an empty space. The energies of the astrological sign will still be absorbed, but not a lot will happen in a dramatic way. All of us have periods of time when we are required to stop and just be. Life is not about continual change; we cannot learn our life lessons if we are rushing through life. These quiet periods are required for rest and thought. That is not to say nothing will happen, but you will not be motivated to activate any planets or area of your charts. Any influence will come from outside, from others.

Can you feel the influence of the age point by sign? Is it activating any planet? By analysing your own chart, you can understand how subtle age point can be—and also how accurate.

## Four

# THE OUTER PLANETS

*T*his lesson will introduce the final planets (with the exception of Saturn, which has chapter 7 to itself a little later on). For now, we are going to concentrate on Uranus, Neptune, and Pluto. Because they are slow-moving planets and because they are so far away from Earth, entire generations have them in the same astrological sign. Because of this, they are generally interpreted by the house they are in instead of by the sign.

When interpreting a chart, the house position of the outer planets is extremely important because they are so effective at their jobs. And their jobs? In short, whichever house they are situated in, Uranus will disrupt, Neptune will confuse and muddy the waters, and Pluto will desire to control that area of life (house).

Conjunctions are when two planets are so close together that their energies combine. If these outer planets are conjunct a personal planet, they will affect the way it acts quite significantly. When two or more outer planets conjunct each other, they show more generalised, long-term trends in your life, but if they connect closely to a personal planet, the effect is immediate and real.

Whole books have been written about each of the outer planets, yet the effect of each one in a chart can be summed up fairly succinctly.

# Uranus
♅ ⛢

**Affects:** Individuality, freedom of thought, flashes of inspiration, unpredictability

Uranus is the ruler of Aquarius, and knowing this will help you understand how Uranus works. It is the planet of unpredictable, sudden change. Any house it occupies will be one in which the individual is unreliable, unpredictable, and prone to sudden changes of direction. It wants to be free of constraint, so if restrictions come along, they will prompt Uranus to act. Too much boring routine and Uranus will shake things up.

Where is the symbol for Uranus in your chart? Check this out, as it is very important. If it is very close to another planet (within three degrees) it is said to be conjunct, and this will make the planet it is close to behave unpredictably as well. The affected planet will still reflect its own astrological sign's way of feeling, acting, or speaking, but being conjunct Uranus will add a dash of the unpredictable to it.

Someone with Uranus conjunct the sun, no matter what astrological sign the sun is in, will occasionally do unpredictable things and disappear if people try to hem them in. Conjunct the moon, it makes people emotionally unpredictable. Uranus conjunct Mercury will be someone whose speech is direct and unpredictable, someone who sometimes makes random, shocking remarks, or someone who says things deliberately to upset the apple cart. Conjunct Venus, Uranus will create a desire for excitement in love and a need to shock with the choice of partner. Uranus conjunct Mars will make people erratic in their ambitions and life choices, liable to choose something unusual or that shocks or surprises others. If Jupiter is conjunct Uranus, there is an overpowering need to be personally free. It also creates the desire to study and explore all areas of life. So great is the need to explore all life has to offer that sticking to routines and timetables is impossible. This is indicative of the explorer, who goes into uncharted territory, either literally, mentally, or emotionally.

For example, let's take a moon in Gemini and put it conjunct Uranus. This person would have two sides to their emotions because Gemini's symbol is the twins; they would be able to switch from being chatty and friendly to being quite detached and verbally cutting. But, to add further complication to someone already emotionally unpredictable, the moon is conjunct Uranus. This person would still act the same way as a moon in Gemini, but Uranus would make an emotional switch a sudden, unexpected event. A moon in Gemini conjunct Uranus would have unpredictable mood swings and, because Uranus needs to be free, they would be impossible to emotionally pin down.

Look at your birth chart. What house is Uranus in? Is it conjunct any planets?

# Neptune
## ♆

**Affects:** Universal love, humility, spirituality, selflessness, confusion/deception

Neptune rules Pisces. To understand how Neptune works, remember the symbol of Pisces, which is two fish swimming in opposite directions. Think of each fish as an idea. One minute this idea seems good, so the fish begins swimming in one direction—but then along comes the second fish (idea) going in the *other* direction, and that seems good too. How can you choose which fish (idea) to follow when both seem good? Also imagine the fish are swimming in murky water. With no signposts and being effectively blind and deaf, the only thing to do is tune in to their intuition and let that guide them. This is how Pisces functions. So, Neptune and the sign it rules, Pisces, are unable to make logical decisions—or any decisions, for that matter.

Neptune muddies the water and confuses things. It makes things dreamy and idealistic. No matter how logical a planet is, if it is conjunct Neptune, it becomes vague and indecisive. But it also becomes compassionate and understanding and, often, psychic.

To go into more detail, no matter what sign the sun is in, conjunct Neptune will make that person more vague, indecisive, and dreamy. Moon conjunct Neptune people are emotionally compassionate and sweet, but they are unable to make good emotional choices because of their blindness to the bad in people. Mars conjunct Neptune will lose all of its drive; it's like dunking a hot iron in cold water. Those with Mars conjunct Neptune find it hard to be ambitious and driven and often rely on gut instinct. Jupiter is already an expansive planet, full of the joy of life, but conjunct Neptune it takes the ideals and imagination to a higher level. Jupiter conjunct Neptune suggests a highly spiritually evolved person who might seek to change the world for the better. On a personal level, they are incredibly kindhearted and charitable.

Imagine someone has Neptune conjunct Mercury, the planet of communication. When conjunct Neptune, Mercury becomes vague and indecisive. Mercury conjunct Neptune simply cannot work in the logical, clearheaded way it is meant to.

There is an idealistic side to Neptune. It always sees the good and prefers not to accept that bad exists, so the word *deception* is often ascribed to Neptune. But Neptune—the ruler of the twelfth house and of Pisces—is a spiritual planet and cannot consciously deceive. Being so forgiving and accepting, it can be easily deceived by others. It also often deceives itself because of an inability to distinguish fantasy from reality; everything is possible to Neptune, who rises to great spiritual heights and only sees the best in others.

Where is Neptune in your birth chart, and how does it affect you?

## Pluto
♇ ♇

**Affects:** Transformation, intensity, rebirth, obsession, passion, controlling power

Pluto is the ruler of Scorpio, and we all know Scorpio is no pussycat! Mars was originally the ruler of both Aries and Scorpio, but Pluto was discovered at the same time as nuclear power was first harnessed, in the 1930s, so Pluto was assigned to be Scorpio's ruling planet, and it is linked to nuclear war.

The house Pluto occupies shows where an individual wants to be in control. If Pluto is in the tenth house of career, that person will want to be the absolute boss, or they will want to work for themselves and not answer to anyone else. If Pluto is in the fourth house, that person will want to be in control of the household. They will want to make the decisions and be deferred to. Whatever house Pluto occupies is one in which the individual will not take orders or direction from others.

Pluto also likes to control, just like the sign it rules, Scorpio. Another word for this is *manipulation*. Pluto watches and waits, then subtly manipulates people and situations to bring them to a position Pluto/Scorpio would prefer.

Remember, Scorpio is the ruler of the eighth house, and this house is all about *other people's* emotions, sexuality, and money.

Conjunct another planet, Pluto will encourage that planet to become stronger, more forceful, and more controlling—in effect, Scorpio-like. (The word *forceful* in this context does not mean physical power, it means determination of mind.) No matter what planet Pluto is conjunct, it will imbue that planet with depth, strength of character, and passion.

If Pluto is conjunct the sun, it gives extra depth and passion to the personality. Conjunct the moon makes for an emotionally passionate person. Pluto conjunct Mercury gives tremendous power to a person's words. Pluto conjunct Mars will infuse the life force and drive with a steely determination to succeed. Conjunct Jupiter, Pluto imbues the individual with the need to have power and influence and to make their mark on the world.

Is Pluto conjunct another planet in your chart? In what house is it trying to exert its influence?

## Other Planet Conjunctions

While we are looking at conjunctions, be aware that conjunctions of planets are quite common in a chart. Some charts have a group of planets focused in one area.

Remember, planets that are conjunct are only combining their energy in the same area; they are homing in on that house. Check what the house oversees and it will be easy to determine which aspects of life hold an individual's interest. For example, someone with a conjunction in the first house might be expending all their energy on how they present themselves; a conjunction in the third house might lead to a deep interest in communication, teaching, or learning. Don't be daunted when you see planets together. Take it one step at a time and work through things logically.

The sun conjunct another planet often eclipses it. However, assuming both planets are in the same astrological sign, they can work together in harmony. For example, someone with the sun conjunct the moon will tend to present their sun sign traits more so than their emotional moon aspects because the sun is a more powerful and forceful planet. Yet, if you get to know them better, the moon sign is able to be perceived. The moon sign was always there, but you were initially blinded by the brightness of the sun.

If the moon is conjunct another planet, it will make the other planet more emotional. If Mercury is conjunct another planet, it will make it more verbal. Venus conjunct a planet will make it more loving and Mars will make it more driven. If Jupiter is conjunct another planet, it will inflate it and give it a greater sense of importance.

Again, there are swathes of information about conjunctions on the internet, and there are many books written about them. But like all aspects of astrology, the basics are simple and straightforward. Once you understand the basic principle of a conjunction, it is easy to apply it in any birth chart.

# Five
## SECTIONS OF A BIRTH CHART

*H*ave a look at the following image. Imagine this is your birth chart. You might recognise the symbols outside the chart: AC (for ascendant), IC (roots), DC (descendant), and MC (midheaven). We call these *angles*. Note we have divided the chart into four quadrants.

An individual's inner motivations can be analysed depending on where the planets are in the chart: in the top or bottom sections, on the left or right, or even in one of the four sections (quadrants). Let's start with defining each quadrant.

## The Four Quadrants

The bottom left quadrant—the quarter section from the AC to IC—is called the *impulsive quadrant*. This is because planets here react impulsively. People with most (or a lot) of their planets in this quadrant tend to act without thinking. They do what they want without taking other people into account. This is not to say they are destructive or cruel, but they don't think about their actions. They just do things automatically.

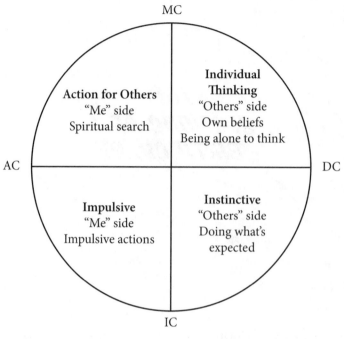

Individual Thinking

MC

**Action for Others**
"Me" side
Spiritual search

**Individual Thinking**
"Others" side
Own beliefs
Being alone to think

AC

DC

**Impulsive**
"Me" side
Impulsive actions

**Instinctive**
"Others" side
Doing what's expected

IC

Collective Community

The quadrant on the other side at the bottom, from the IC to the DC, is referred to as the *instinctive quadrant*. Planets here are more conscious of other people. They act on instinct, following the rules set out by their country, society, or community. They do the things expected of them by others— go to school, graduate college, marry, have children, get a job, and so forth— all without questioning why they are doing it; it is expected of them, it is what people do, therefore it is what they do.

The next section goes from the DC to the MC. This is called the *individual thinking quadrant*. If people have planets here, at the top of the chart, they are rising above what's expected of them. They enjoy thinking for themselves. They develop their own ideas about the meaning of life and form their own personal philosophies. Most people here have a wider perspective of life and a farsighted vision, and they do not want to mix in with the busy collective community at the bottom of the chart. They don't necessarily feel they are better than others, just slightly removed from everything. This feeling of being better than everyone else can occur, of course, but it isn't a given.

The final section is called the *action for others quadrant*. People with planets here are self-aware and conscious of the connectedness of all life; they see themselves as only one small part linked to the whole of humanity. They like to be of use and to help those less fortunate, whether that is by sitting on committees, supporting charities, or encouraging religious and spiritual growth. If they have more than two personal planets in the twelfth house, they may not feel actively drawn to partake in life. They seek their own spiritual meaning, but very often they end up doing charitable work simply because of their compassion for others.

Check your own chart. Make a note of how many planets are in each quadrant. Where is the emphasis? Does this new knowledge bring greater understanding of your motives?

## The Top and Bottom Halves

Now that we have analysed the four quadrants, let's look at the top and bottom halves.

In chapter 3, we covered age point, so we know that the first half of a birth chart covers the thirty-six years of life. The whole lower half of a birth chart, below the AC/DC line, is called the *collective community*. These are the years we endeavour to find our place in society and to do the things expected of us. We are part of the collective identity and our community.

People with the majority of their planets here are happy within their own environment. They do what is expected of them. They need the security of their family and friends around them. They are happy to make a significant contribution to their community—anything from volunteering at schools and the workplace, running a local club, driving people here and there, etc. They strive to maintain the continuity of the collective community by being an active member of it.

The whole upper section, above the AC/DC line, is called the *individual thinking area* because those with planets at the top of their chart think for themselves. They do not necessarily believe what they are told; they prefer to find their own answers. They are not trapped within other people's expectations of them.

People with planets in this sector don't want to get involved; they perceive the collective community as noisy, busy, and chaotic. A university professor is the perfect example of this. Professors sit alone in an office writing articles for elite magazines or editing specialised books, occasionally dipping into the collective community by teaching a few classes, but always returning to the peace of the individual thinking quadrant. They like being alone to think, write, and learn.

Look again at your chart. Are most of the planets at the bottom? Are most of the planets at the top? Or are they scattered between the two? If they are scattered between the two halves, this means you are versatile and can dip into both areas.

## The Left and Right Sides

We can also interpret the left and right sides of a birth chart.

The whole left side of the chart, from the IC to MC, is known as the *"me" area*. Therefore, if a birth chart has all or most of the planets on the left, that person will not need other people. They are happy alone and are quite self-contained, maybe even reclusive or hermit-like if all the planets are in the upper left half. People with a scattering of planets all down the left side of their birth chart may choose jobs that are away from the public eye, like working in a prison or hospital, or they might decide to enter religious or spiritual institutions. They may choose work that takes them away for long periods of time or prefer to work from home or in lone occupations. Alternatively, they might have ordinary jobs, but they would ideally have an office to themselves. Regardless of their profession, they will always spend most of their free time on their own.

They might choose not to marry or have children. Certainly, if they do, it will not be easy for them to relate to their partners and children. Their partner may take care of a lot of the day-to-day work and run the household.

If every personal planet is on the "me" side, this means the individual will have problems relating to others. The moon here on this side of the chart, especially, means emotionally bonding with another will be difficult.

At the opposite end of the spectrum is someone with all or most of their planets on the right-hand side of the chart. The entire right side of the chart, from the IC to MC, is known as the *"others" area*. These individuals desperately need other people. What other people think and say and expect from them will form the whole structure of their lives.

Someone with all their planets on the right-hand side is unable to function alone. They will marry or find partners early in life, and if a partner leaves, they might feel suicidal. Without other people, they are lost and have no inner resources.

So, are you "me" sided or "others" sided? Are you happier in the collective community or up in the individual thinking sector? Can you see how enlightening this knowledge is?

# *Six*
# *ASPECTS AND*
# *ASPECT PATTERNS*

*T*he coloured lines inside a chart are called *aspect lines*. These are con-
nections between the planets. Earlier, I recommended choosing a Huber
house system to create a birth chart, and this was specifically because Huber
uses only red, blue, and green aspect lines and is therefore clearer and easier to interpret. Other house systems are fine, but there may be different
coloured aspect lines and symbols in the birth chart that could be confusing.
I am working with a Huber chart, and I highly recommend you do too.

Before we go into detail, have a quick look at the following chart.

| Aspect | Symbol | Angle | Description |
|---|---|---|---|
| Conjunction | ☌ | 0° | Planets within a few degrees of each other |
| Semi-sextile | ⊻ | 30° | One sign apart |
| Sextile | ✶ | 60° | Two signs apart |
| Square | □ | 90° | Three signs apart |

| Aspect | Symbol | Angle | Description |
|--------|--------|-------|-------------|
| Trine | △ | 120° | Four signs apart |
| Quincunx | ⚻ | 150° | Five signs apart |
| Opposition | ☍ | 180° | Six signs apart |

We all know the moon's energy has the power to affect the flow of Earth's oceans and that gravity, an unseen energy, holds us all to the surface of our own planet. Aspects take this idea and apply it. All the planets have energies. The closer the planet to Earth, the stronger its effect. The sun is obviously the largest and most powerful.

The degrees on a birth chart are indicated by little black lines on the inside of the ring that shows the astrological signs. Each of the signs is thirty degrees (thirty little black lines). So to know how many degrees two planets are from each other, you simply count the little black lines between them.

In general, it is accepted that the sun and moon energies, being so powerful, can extend up to about nine degrees (nine of those little black lines). This figure is slightly lower for the other planets, right down to two or three degrees for the outer planets. In other words, if one planet is at three degrees Aries and another at five degrees Libra, they would make an aspect to each other—in this case, an opposition.

The Huber birth chart you created online will have already worked out these aspects, so you don't have to. As discussed previously, a conjunction is the strongest aspect and is shown on a chart by a block of colour between the planets affected. Usually, orange is used. The colours used for other aspects are red, blue, and green. Other house system charts will use different colours, so if you haven't already got a Huber chart, it is best to print one out now. Sometimes even the Huber chart will show other colours.

If you've created a birth chart using a program, you can easily change the colours for the aspects under the program's settings. Choose orange for conjunctions, red for oppositions and squares, blue for trines and sextiles, and green for the semi-sextile and the quincunx. Their names will be given as well as their symbol, so it should be easy.

# Red Aspects

Red aspects show energy. There are typically two red aspects in a chart, the square and the opposition.

The square (written in shorthand as literally a square) is energy that can be put to work. Think of Martian energy. The planets connected by the square are energised, and their combined energy can get things done. A square is a contact between planets ninety degrees apart. Each sign is thirty degrees, so a square is three astrological signs. For example, if the sun is twenty degrees in Taurus and the moon is twenty-two degrees in Leo, they would form a square.

Have a look at your birth chart and see if you can find the short red line that indicates a square. Think how it might affect the two planets connected in this way.

The only other red aspect is the opposition. These are the long red lines that stretch right across a chart. An opposition is energy that is blocked off. The energy is there, but which end of the opposition should it be directed toward? It is impossible to use both planets together.

For example, if the sun and moon are in opposition, bringing one's self-expression and emotions together is impossible, so these people never feel whole. They are either expressing their sun (their will) or their moon (their emotions); they cannot use both at the same time. The houses affected are very important. In this scenario, the individual will want to express who they are via the house their sun is in, but emotionally, they will feel more comfortable in the opposite house. This tension is rarely overcome. Most likely, the individual would just get used to always feeling a bit at odds. It creates a sense of discontent that is subtle—the vague feeling that no matter where they are or what they are doing, they are never truly themselves.

Some charts have no oppositions. These are people who are able to integrate their energies more fully. But be aware that tension creates drive. Very often, those with more difficult aspects strive harder to create the life they want, while a lack of tension can create a more relaxed (lazy) attitude to life. Like everything, there are positives and negatives to having or not having oppositions in a birth chart.

An opposition line that cuts right across a chart from the AC to the DC (or from the MC to the IC) will cut that person off from wanting any contact with the area of life it blocks. This is only an issue when all of the planets are on one side; in that case, the empty section is the area the person is afraid to go. If you see this in a birth chart, look back at chapter 5 to remind yourself what each section of the chart means.

Do you have an opposition in your chart? Have a think about how the energies of the planets involved might be affected. Use your knowledge of each planet's energies and the houses they are in. This is the best way to get a handle on aspects and their influence. But don't get too confused or overwhelmed trying to work it out. The more you look at birth charts, the clearer things will become. You can always come back to aspects at a later date.

## Blue Aspects

Blue aspects show someone's ability to relax and have fun. They are an easy aspect. Too much blue in a chart, though, and the individual may lack drive. Too little blue and the individual will find it hard to relax and chill.

The shortest of the blue aspects is the sextile, which has a Venus feel. A sextile links planets two astrological signs apart in a harmonious way, enabling them to work together comfortably. Very often, this link shows a natural talent for something that requires only a little bit of effort to develop it further.

The longer blue aspect is the trine. This is a link between planets that are four astrological signs apart. A trine has a Jupiter feel. It shows an inherent talent that needs little or no work.

Look at your birth chart. Do you have sextiles in your birth chart? What about trines? Look at the planets and the houses involved. Can you see how these energies work together in your own life?

## Green Aspects

Green aspects are "seeking, questioning, doubting" lines. People with green aspects keep an open mind and come up with their own answers to the mysteries of life. People without any green aspects have no interest in why humanity is here or what our purpose is. People without green aspects believe we just *are*, and that's that. They have a very black-and-white attitude with no shades of grey.

The shorter green line is called the semi-sextile. A semi-sextile links planets one astrological sign apart. It absorbs facts and information from the specific area of life (house) the semi-sextile covers. This is done instinctively and requires no effort.

The quincunx is the longer green line. This line suggests a desire to reach the whole truth. It involves a conscious decision to seek and find, and as such, it creates a sort of divine discontent.

Take a look at your birth chart. Do you have a semi-sextile or quincunx? People who want to learn astrology and other esoteric subjects often have green aspects, especially the quincunx.

## Colour Balance

The balance of coloured lines is important. Ideally, a birth chart would have all three colours. This shows we are able to expend energy (red), search for answers (green), and relax and enjoy life (blue).

People without red aspects—the square and opposition—have no drive to energise their planets. They think (green) and they are able to relax and enjoy life (blue), but they take no action unless it is absolutely necessary. People might describe them, at best, as dreamy. At worst, lazy.

People without blue aspects—the sextile and trine—do not have the ability to relax, so they relax by being active, whether through sports or activities. Red and green aspects create tension and irritability. This inability to relax creates a restless person, always on the go—if not physically, then mentally. They are unable to switch off.

People without green aspects—the semi-sextile and quincunx—do not question their existence. They work and rest, but they do not think deeply about life. It is common to have fewer green aspects in a chart, so only one or two green aspects is still an important indicator of awareness of the bigger picture.

This colour balance is even more important than the interpretation of the aspects. A quick glance at a chart will immediately show you a lot about a person based on which aspect colours are there—and which aren't.

# Aspect Patterns

Very often, but not always, the aspect lines form a pattern. Some of these patterns are quite distinct and are worth noting. There are quite a few different aspect patterns, but for now, let's look at the most important ones.

Be aware that some books or astrologers may give these aspect patterns a slightly different name, so concentrate on the patterns and what they are telling you about yourself or others (if doing someone else's chart) rather than the actual name—although they are often very similar.

## Red Aspect Patterns

The first two are made up of all red aspect lines. As we know, red aspect lines are energy. A person with either of these patterns will be hardworking and driven.

### SQUARE

This pattern is formed when there are four square aspects and two oppositions, so it is an all-red pattern. It is sometimes referred to as the grand cross. When someone has this pattern in their chart, they work hard to achieve their goals. And when blocked in one area, they can easily move to another. They don't need to rest. They are often workaholics.

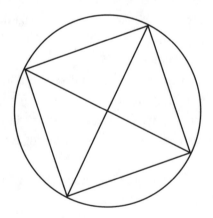

### T-SQUARE/EFFICIENCY TRIANGLE

People with this pattern will go looking for work even when there is none. However, unlike the square aspect pattern, they will stop now and then to rest. It helps if there are some blue aspect lines in the chart; these will be needed to slow them down. The energy is usually expended using the planet at the apex of the triangle.

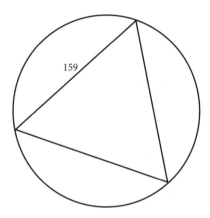

## Blue Aspect Patterns

The all-blue aspect patterns are the large and small talent triangles. Blue aspect patterns often denote a natural, inherited ability. It is important to have some red in the chart (whether this is from planets in fire signs or from red aspect lines). Otherwise, a blue-dominant person could be so relaxed that they don't actively use their talent in the world.

### LARGE TALENT TRIANGLE/GRAND TRINE

This large talent triangle is composed of three trines. The houses linked by the three trines are the areas of talent. This talent is recognised (known about) by the individual.

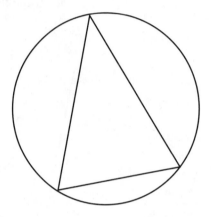

### SMALL TALENT TRIANGLE

This smaller aspect pattern of a trine and two sextiles indicates a talent that needs to be worked on. Because it is all blue, action will be gradual. The planet and house at the triangle apex will show the talent and the area where it can be expressed.

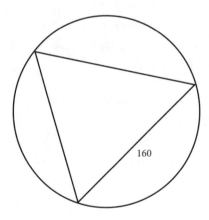

## Red and Green Aspect Patterns

Red and green aspect patterns create tension. As we have seen with aspects colours, red and green aspects create irritability and irritation. There are two important patterns to note: the irritation triangle and irritation rectangle.

### THE IRRITATION TRIANGLE

This is formed when an opposition and quincunx are joined together at one end with a semi-sextile so that two green aspects are linked to a red.

Red and green produce irritation in an individual. They are aware of things (green) but find it hard to adapt to the demands of others. This results in sudden anger. They cannot suppress their irritation. It must be verbalised so that the tension can be released.

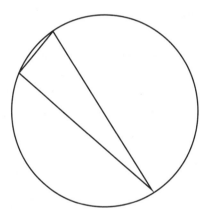

### IRRITATION RECTANGLE

This is an extremely difficult aspect pattern where two oppositions are surrounded in green lines, two quincunxes and two semi-sextiles. These people are extremely sensitive. Things will hurt them very much, but outwardly they will pretend not to care. Their green aspects notice every hurt, but they don't want to admit it. The resulting tension produces phobias and fears, and this can result in addictions (likely to be drugs or alcohol) to escape their sensitivities.

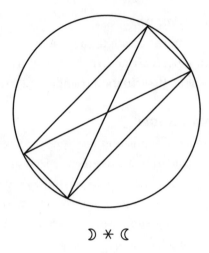

☽ ⚹ ☾

Does your chart have any of these aspect patterns? Can you understand how they work in your life?

There are quite a few aspect patterns. In fact, any aspect lines that form a pattern can be assessed using the knowledge gained thus far about aspect lines and colours, and these assessments will likely be fairly accurate. If you'd like to research other aspect patterns, there are plenty of articles and books written about them.

Part II
DIVING DEEPER

## Seven
## *SATURN*
## ♄

**A**ffects: Discipline, authority, caution, restriction, restraint, fear area
Saturn has a chapter all to itself. This is because it is now thought of as a karmic planet. I say now because as the human race grows in a spiritual sense, they seek more meaning from life. Astrology used to be all about prediction, but it is now also used as a psychological tool for understanding ourselves and our life purpose. Astrology has always had many layers, but we can only grasp them if we are open to accepting there is more to life than the physical, material aspects. It is now accepted that Saturn shows us our karmic life lessons.

The inherent intimation in karma is that we live more than one life, and in each we learn from our previous mistakes. This premise is for each person to decide, but suffice to say that Saturn's position usually resonates very strongly with people, so it is hard to dismiss such compelling evidence.

Saturn rules the sign of Capricorn and, in traditional Capricorn fashion, hard work and lifelong lessons are necessary before any gains or rewards are achieved in the area (house) Saturn is placed.

Saturn is viewed as the bringer of restrictions, obstacles, and limitations, and its lessons are learnt over a whole lifetime. It is sometimes described as a person's fear area. Certainly, the area (house) Saturn occupies is one in which an individual will have the most difficulty—yet confronting and mastering those fears is considered a karmic life lesson.

To repeat, Saturn offers a lifetime of situations that allow an individual to confront (or avoid dealing with) the issues covered by the house where Saturn resides. There is no right or wrong way to handle it, but awareness brings understanding, which is why simply knowing about Saturn can be enlightening and releasing.

When looking at Saturn in a birth chart, make sure to pay attention to both the sign and the house it is in to fully understand Saturn's message. For example, if Saturn is in Pisces in the second house, you would read the following sections on "Saturn in Pisces or the Twelfth House" *and* "Saturn in Taurus or the Second House."

## Saturn in Aries or the First House

The first house is the ascendant and how we present ourselves to others. It is our mask, our personal disguise that we use until we feel able to let strangers get to know us better. When Saturn is here, in the first house, it is in a particularly strong position—even more so if it is close to, or right on, the ascendant itself—because it will hamper the individual's ability to fully relate to others. Saturn will make the individual very cautious about (maybe even afraid of) allowing others access to their inner selves.

The sign of Aries rules the first house, and Aries is all about oneself. Aries talks about themselves and their plans, and they have a childlike enthusiasm and embrace of all life has to offer. But Saturn prevents this natural enthusiasm. It suppresses it, resulting in a fear of speaking up for themselves and of pushing themselves forward. Thus, people with Saturn in Aries or the first house come across as quite shy, modest people who avoid the limelight or any situation where they may be called on to emerge from the crowd. Even though the ascendant is already a mask, Saturn gives an extra layer of wariness and prevents natural and open relating.

When Saturn is in Aries or the first house, it makes the individual fearful of confrontation. They believe they have no right to argue their point. This leaves them vulnerable to being manipulated and controlled by others.

Saturn rules the physical body, and all these suppressed feelings are often released through physical activity. Physically active people usually have a prominent Saturn, either on or near the AC. (It's also common for physically active people to have a Capricorn ascendant because Saturn rules Capricorn.)

The good news is, Saturn is synonymous with old age, acquiring wisdom, and lifetime learning. So, as an individual ages, Saturn will gradually provide them with more confidence founded on a lifetime of experience. People with Saturn in Aries or the first house gradually learn how to present themselves and how to speak up. Instead of appearing fearful, they will show themselves as quietly serious and responsible. Other people subconsciously pick up on this and ask them for advice, deferring to their suggestions. Saturn is the wise elder, the teacher, and this is what people eventually perceive when meeting someone with a Saturn in Aries or the first house.

Saturn is all about learning lessons and, in this position, it is teaching the individual that it is a waste of energy to confront others. It is far better to find a way to disarm an enemy or competitor. As they age, these individuals learn the right way to handle people who come into their lives, especially if they are intrusive or disruptive.

## Saturn in Taurus or the Second House

Saturn's karmic lessons in the second house (which is ruled by Taurus) centre around how we feel about and act toward money and possessions.

With Saturn in Taurus or the second house, people judge themselves by what they own rather than on their abilities; not on who they are but on what they have. This need for financial security is an overriding motivation in their lives, with all their actions based on the desire to have more security. For them, security is represented by money in the bank, owning houses and land, or even acquiring highly valued works of art—possessions, in effect.

Very often, this relentless pursuit of money is because they suffered poverty or hardship when growing up. They now see money as the way out of their current existence, a passport to a better life in the material sense. Rolling up their sleeves and working hard is not a problem for them; they are more than willing to do what it takes. But this becomes their entire focus. Gaining money and possessions is the underlying focus behind every action they take. Even if they manage to surround themselves with material goods and have money in the bank, the fear remains—but now it is a fear of losing all they have worked so hard for.

Saturn is the teacher. It teaches that the more we cling to something or someone, the more likely we are to lose it/them. There is a saying that if you chase money, it runs away from you. This is often the case with this position. No matter how hard they work or what routes they take to create security for themselves, one way or another, it eludes them.

Saturn's lesson here is to teach an individual to find their own values and not the world's ideal (and solely material) image of success. They must learn that there is more to life than money and possessions, that values and ideals also have a place, that material possessions do not mean true security, and that happiness cannot truly be found in a new purchase or in a stable bank balance.

## Saturn in Gemini or the Third House

Saturn's karmic lessons in the third house or in the sign of Gemini are all about how an individual speaks and communicates.

Saturn here creates a feeling of intellectual inadequacy and an inability to express personal ideas and feelings. It might be that the individual was ridiculed when they spoke up at home or at school. Regardless, they feel inadequate with words. Speaking up for themselves and sharing their own ideas will be the problem area, especially when it comes to expressing their deep emotions.

This usually means the individual makes extra sure of their facts before they speak out. They might tend to hide their personal feelings behind facts and information. If they do that, they think, no one can ridicule or embarrass them. Yet, the more they hide behind facts, the more they lose the ability to express their true selves through speech.

Because Saturn is good at research and never gives up, this placement can produce people who can make breakthroughs in research or science. But this is a catch-22 because they find themselves unable to communicate normally.

In truth, these individuals are often so cerebral that people have difficulty speaking about the ordinary things in life with them.

Saturn in Gemini or the third house creates a fear of communicating normally without hiding behind intellectual subjects. It is seen in those who are happier in a business meeting than talking to friend, or happier writing an academic paper than chatting at the bar. Life will teach them how to balance the two, though Saturn's fear never entirely dissipates. There will always be a slight reservation about expressing their innermost feelings.

## Saturn in Cancer or the Fourth House

If Saturn is in the sign of Cancer or in the fourth house, its karmic lessons are about the home and family background.

The ideal image of the home and family is one of mutual love and support; Saturn here suggests this was not the case for these people. For whatever reason, that warmth and love was lacking. As people tend to emulate their own family, those with Saturn here find it hard to go on to create their own family unit, mainly because they have no idea how to go about it.

An individual's background issues could have many and various causes: a single-parent family where the lone parent was out working, a real or perceived rejection by a parent, or just that the parents were too busy to be there when needed. It might be that they were always being evicted or lost their actual home at some point. Any of these things would cause the child to fear this area of life and to over-compensate when they grow up by investing their time and energy in creating something that they feel cannot be taken away from them.

Another effect of Saturn here is the person believing they do not need anyone else. They survived a difficult childhood and managed fine; they take this feeling through life with them, seeing rejection as proof they are unlovable. Thus, they can end up living alone, pretending everything is all right and that they are okay.

Their life lessons will centre around family relationships. Gradually, Saturn will teach them how to rise above the coldness they faced to reassess what happened from an adult perspective. People with Saturn in Cancer or the fourth house must accept and acknowledge that they are lovable and deserve the right to have a happy, warm home just as much as anyone else.

## Saturn in Leo or the Fifth House

Saturn's karmic lessons in Leo or the fifth house focus on how an individual expresses themselves through artistic endeavours, children, love affairs, and general life enjoyment.

Saturn in this house suppresses the natural exuberance. In a way, this is more about self-esteem than anything else; no matter how gifted or clever these people are, they don't feel worthy of admiration and praise. This probably stems from childhood experiences of not being appreciated, their gifts not being recognised, or their efforts dismissed or ridiculed.

This creates a feeling within them of not being worthy of love. And if they find it hard to love themselves, how can others? This results in them being defensive and withdrawn. Saturn in Leo or the fifth house people tend to have an "I'm fine" attitude when actually, they are not; they feel unloved and unappreciated no matter what they do.

Saturn in the fifth house often indicates a difficulty in having children. The result is that they feel inadequate because they cannot have children. If they do have children, something about the child brings restrictions, resulting in a lack of ability to embrace a joyful life for one reason or another. Sometimes they consciously choose a childless life, so they lose that connection to the joyous, spontaneous, and fun aspects of life that come with children.

Saturn in Leo people desperately need admiration because Leos get their sense of inner worth from others' admiration and praise, which inspires them to work even harder. Saturn here will make them feel they can never attain that, which becomes a self-fulfilling prophesy. They will find themselves envying others who (they think) have more, are loved more, or are admired more.

Saturn in Leo or the fifth house is teaching an individual how to express themselves—how to show who they really are without requiring the acceptance and admiration of others. Only then can they find a truly fulfilling love because they can open themselves to others. As life progresses, they will realise that the praise of others is not necessary to their own self-esteem.

## Saturn in Virgo or the Sixth House

Saturn's karmic lessons in the sixth house or in the sign of Virgo are all about service to others in a work environment. Virgo also rules bodily health.

Virgo is a hard taskmaster, and the sixth house is a place of physical service, of rolling up one's sleeves and doing the menial tasks. These people already like order and neatness, but Saturn ensures they are overconcerned with rules and regulations—obsessed almost. Rules become so essential for their well-being that any deviation from this path is greeted with fear, leaving them constantly in a state of anxiety that something awful is about to happen to their health, their job, or their life.

For those with Saturn in Virgo or the sixth house, routine and order equate to safety. Many of these people work in jobs they are unhappy in, yet they won't leave them because they know the routine; nothing unplanned or unknown will upset their ordered lives.

Saturn here creates an inability to say no to anyone. In the end, they give so much of themselves that they become exhausted. Under their hardworking exterior, they resent the amount of work they do and may constantly complain without doing anything to alter their situation. To overcompensate, they focus on health and may follow strict diet regimes and/or punishing exercise schedules. It will be an easy step to hypochondria.

Saturn here is trying to teach the true meaning of balance—to serve willingly with joy—and to maintain the physical body without recourse to extremes.

## Saturn in Libra or the Seventh House

Saturn's karmic lessons in the seventh house or in the sign of Libra are all about partnerships, one-to-one relationships, and marriage. As discussed in chapter 3, the seventh house reflects what we are looking for in a partner.

Traditionally, Saturn here leads to problems forming long-term relationships and/or marriage difficulties—but these difficulties are perceived as coming from others, from their partner. Those with Saturn in Libra or the seventh house lay the blame at the feet of others, not realising they have the problem.

In effect, they expect their relationships to fail. They fear being emotionally or physically dependent on anyone else. Those with Saturn in Libra or the seventh house do marry and have relationships, but they are not committed heart and soul to the union. They remain aloof, keeping something of themselves back. They may deliberately (but subconsciously) choose someone who is older, someone who may need care, or someone who is bound to disappoint or reject them in some way. They set up their own future difficulties in their choice.

As they go through life, Saturn will force them to confront relationship issues, to question why they chose their partner in the first place, and to realize that *they* have the problem, not their partner. Only then can they form a happy partnership. And, like all Saturn placements, this will come later in life, after many years of soul-searching.

## Saturn in Scorpio or the Eighth House

There are many old adages about Saturn in this house or sign. Nothing about the eighth house or the sign of Scorpio is straightforward or clear. Traditionally, Saturn here means death in old age (seen as a positive, of course) and the denial of inheritances (a negative). This house is associated with death and money.

Money—and in the eighth house, we are referring to other people's money —can be a bone of contention. Many people with Saturn in Scorpio or the eighth house have a fear of losing financial support, whether from their parents, marriage, or business partners. They may feel financially restricted by their partners or may suffer financially after a divorce or parting. Oftentimes, it is a combination of things. Money and sex have always been part of a game of hidden power, and never more so that when the eighth house and Scorpio are involved.

People with Saturn in Scorpio or the eighth house may have problems connected to their childhood. They may have been abused (physically, emotionally, or sexually) or felt rejected as a child. Either way, they were probably trapped, unable to leave the situation that caused so much distress.

Because our upbringing plays a crucial role in our development, this means relating to others is not straightforward for these people. In fact, they often end up recreating those painful childhood situations by marrying someone they do not actually physically want or choosing someone who undermines or belittles them, depending on the abuse they suffered. This creates a feeling of emotional isolation.

For those with Saturn in Scorpio or the eighth house, life and its lessons centre around whom they choose to give themselves to and why. It is also important for them to free themselves by becoming financially independent.

This often happens later in life because Saturn's lessons are lifelong. Scorpio, the sign of rebirth, is a beacon of hope that this can be achieved.

## Saturn in Sagittarius or the Ninth House

Saturn's karmic lessons in the ninth house or in the sign of Sagittarius are all about learning taken to a higher level, to a higher consciousness. It's about intuition, insight, and the search for truth. This can involve physical journeys to experience different cultures, or it can be a journey of the mind. Religion, law, philosophy, linguistics, other cultures—all of these can be ways for the individual to find their own answers to the meaning of life. This is basically an esoteric house.

Imagine Saturn, the planet of restriction and structure, here. Saturn will suppress and stunt drive and interest in these areas. People with Saturn in Sagittarius or the ninth house will prefer not to travel. They will deny that religions have any basis or that other cultures have anything enlightening to offer. Esoteric subjects will be of no interest; they will be dismissed as rubbish.

Like every position of Saturn, it is fear that engenders this feeling—fear of foreigners, fear of the chaos that travelling and exploring can create, fear of examining other religions and ideas in case they create any uncertainty in their own traditional beliefs.

Usually, people with Saturn in Sagittarius or the ninth house declare that they believe in nothing at all, but this is only a fear of facing the deeper meaning of life. They refuse to look deeper into subjects that may enlighten them because they do not accept anything out of the traditional way of thinking.

Their life experiences will finally guide them to find their own truth, which is more meaningful than the truth provided by others.

## Saturn in Capricorn or the Tenth House

Saturn's karmic lessons in the tenth house or the sign of Capricorn are to do with career and worldly achievements, those that bring recognition along with status, power, and authority.

The traditional interpretation of Saturn in Capricorn or the tenth house is an outward lack of worldly ambition, a fear of being in the limelight—in effect, a fear of failure, because failure in the tenth house is visible to everyone; it can't be hidden away. Capricorn always strives for the loftiest position in life, so having Saturn here undermines their belief in their own abilities, creating a lack of self-confidence and a fear of striving for what they want.

Consequently, these individuals may follow a more traditional route to success. Saturn restricts, so the climb to power is slow, punctuated with many delays, setbacks, and problems. That is not to say they won't ever reach a position of power—very often, they do. But with Saturn here, they have to be extra cautious to ensure all their actions and dealings are aboveboard. Saturn is always poised to topple them into disgrace if they follow anything other than the most honourable and truthful methods. Any indiscretions or suspicious transactions will come back to haunt them, so they must be doubly circumspect in all they do.

The position of Saturn in Capricorn or the tenth house makes the individual reassess their need for power and status. They are pushed to determine the real meaning of power and status in their life.

## Saturn in Aquarius or the Eleventh House

Saturn's karmic lessons in the eleventh house or the sign of Aquarius are to do with groups and societies.

The eleventh house is in the Action for Others quadrant of the chart and on the "me" side, so there is less interest in relating to others and more emphasis on group friendships and humanitarianism via group activities; to do good often requires joining with others who think similarly.

Saturn in Aquarius or the eleventh house will suppress the desire to join with others. It is not that they do not want to belong (they do, very much!), but they feel out of sync with groups and societies, even familial ones. There is usually one person in every family who comes to events but sits slightly apart, pretending disinterest, leafing through a magazine or playing on their phone; this is a classic Saturn in Aquarius or the eleventh house person. Sensing disinterest, others defer to this isolation. Others do not expect the Saturn in Aquarius or the eleventh house person to fully join in, believing it to be their preference. It isn't. They isolate themselves because of fear, not desire.

The fear in this position of Saturn is one of the most natural: they fear not being accepted. Rather than risk rejection, they pretend they are not bothered. In reality, they wish very much to be part of the group. Maybe as a child they were not accepted by the popular group at school, or perhaps they were always the odd one out at home. (If there is an uneven number of siblings, one is often left out.) Either way, they carry with them a fear of rejection. Their inner voice tells them they don't care, they don't need to be part of the group. The reality is, they long to be included.

Saturn here teaches the individual how to overcome the fear of allowing themselves deep friendships and involvement in social groups. This will come later in life, after many experiences—as do all of Saturn's lessons—but eventually, the individual will take their rightful place in group settings.

## Saturn in Pisces or the Twelfth House

Saturn's karmic lessons in the twelfth house or the sign of Pisces have to do with isolation from the world.

The twelfth house is a place removed from the busy activity of commercial and social life. It deals with religion and faith. Also under its umbrella is any institution that is separate from the world, including hospitals and prisons. Somehow or another, Saturn in Pisces or the twelfth house individuals will have contact with these places, with or without a conscious choice.

The twelfth house and the sign of Pisces are seen as places where people lose their unique identity. Because Saturn creates fear wherever it is, placed here it creates a fear of letting go, of losing individuality, and of having personal control taken away. Yet, very often, these individuals end up experiencing the things they fear. This might mean a prolonged stay in a hospital, a prison sentence, or a deliberate choice to retreat.

People with Saturn in Pisces or the twelfth house will spend their lives afraid of having someone else in charge of their identity, so they strive to become competent and independent. They avoid anyone who threatens to take control away from them. However, as they grow in wisdom and age, people with this position voluntarily choose to live their life for others—eventually. In doing so, they let go of their own uniqueness and see themselves as part of something bigger and more meaningful; they see themselves as part of humankind, which is interlinked in every way.

People with Saturn in Pisces or the twelfth house learn through their enforced isolation. It makes them consider the deeper meaning of life and humanity, and it challenges them to see the bigger picture. Their lessons are truly spiritual.

## Saturn Conjunct Other Planets

Before we leave Saturn, let's look at how it affects other planets in a chart.

As we have already discussed, Saturn brings difficulties and obstacles to the house where it is placed. When it is close to another planet, it will form a conjunction. This means the unique energy of that other planet and how it expresses itself will be affected by Saturn.

Saturn suppresses. It is like having someone sitting on your shoulder and always advising caution. For example, if Saturn is close to the sun in a birth chart, it will affect the sun's ability to shine as fully as it would like. Saturn will be always whispering in the sun's ear to be cautious; it will suppress natural exuberance and make the sun more wary.

Conjunct the moon, Saturn will be advising emotional caution and will affect the individual's ability to fully express their emotions; it will make them refrain from expressing how they feel until they are sure others will accept their feelings. Or it might hamper people's ability to actually feel things deeply; they might respond to things and people in a more conservative, traditional way, unable to give love and emotional support unless it is in a culturally accepted manner.

Conjunct Mercury, it will affect how the person speaks, communicates, and writes. Sometimes it even affects how they read. This will make the individual more cautious and fearful of expressing their opinions and ideas. Thus, they rarely explain how they really feel, either because they have trouble finding the right words or because they are overly concerned with how their words will be received by others. Those with Saturn conjunct Mercury hold their thoughts in, which leads others to believe they are in agreement with them when in fact they might not be. They may only express opinions that are generally accepted—even when those opinions are not really their own belief—in order to not upset the status quo.

When Saturn is conjunct Venus, it will be warning of the danger of being too loving and kind, suggesting the individual may get taken advantage of if they are too obliging. Particularly in women's charts, Saturn prevents the individual from freely giving their love. They may wish to, but they are prevented through fear. Saturn rules Capricorn, which is a traditional sign, so these individuals follow a more traditional path in love even though their natural inclinations may be otherwise. In a man's chart, Saturn conjunct Venus will affect his choice of a female partner; she must be respectable in every way.

Saturn conjunct Mars will affect the individual's ambition and drive, making them more wary of pushing themselves and striving for what they want. Their ambitions may be high, but they may never fully achieve the greatness they desire because they fear taking too many risks. For example, someone with Saturn conjunct Mars may have a small but successful business, but if they get the chance to expand or become global, they likely won't take that risk.

Any planet in close contact with Saturn has a more cautious expression, so Jupiter won't be as liberal and expansive, Uranus won't be so unpredictable, Neptune will be less accepting of others (and more wary of people who might take advantage of their altruistic nature), and Pluto will be prevented from assuming complete control of an area (house).

Saturn's influence is also felt in aspect lines, but generally only in the red aspects. Squares involving Saturn are like having a firm hand on the reins; the other planets will work more cautiously and will take longer to do tasks because there is a karmic learning process involved. Oppositions are more difficult. Whatever planet is opposite Saturn will be restrained. Again, think of the analogy of someone sitting on your shoulder and always advising caution. Saturn subdues the natural inclinations of the planet it is in opposition to. In squares or oppositions, Saturn holds other planets back.

# Eight
## PLANETS ON ANGLES

ngles are the AC, IC, DC, and MC. To recap:

AC stands for the ascendant. It is the line showing the start of the first house.

IC reflects an individual's roots. It is the line showing the start of the fourth house.

DC stands for the descendant. It is the line showing the start of the seventh house.

MC stands for midheaven. It is the line showing the start of the tenth house.

These angles begin the four most important houses. These houses are important because they are the areas of life that most affect us.

The angles (AC, IC, DC, and MC) reflect our ability to handle other people. They affect how we get our way, how we get others to accept us on our own terms, and if we want to control others to achieve our goals. People with planets on the angles are more in control in their relationships. They tend to need less acceptance and approval from others because they feel grounded and capable.

Very few people with planets on angles require praise; they have an inner sense of confidence that gives them a head start in life.

The AC shows how we approach new encounters. The DC shows how we approach close relationships. The MC shows how we deal with group situations. (Do we dominate or direct others?) And the IC shows how we cope with solitude, standing alone and facing the world.

Planets right on the AC line, or very close to it (no more than two degrees away), have a social ease and openness. People with planets here appear straightforward and without guile. There is no desire to ward off people. They make eye contact and are friendly and approachable. This is because they have a clear idea of their own personal abilities and feel no need to prove themselves or to be something they are not, so they appear friendly. But actually, their intimacy is not as warm as it appears. Underneath, they maintain their distance and reserve, watching and analysing. Remember, the AC is a filter, so no matter how friendly they appear, it is a front. Basically, those with a planet on or within a few degrees of the AC *know who they are.*

People with IC planets (and those within a couple of degrees of the IC line) have a firm confidence in themselves and their ability to withstand life's ups and downs. They deal with the stresses of life through their connection to their own inner self and their roots. They are like a tree that sways and bends in the wind but does not break; their roots run deep. Planets here are *at one with their inner self.*

Planets on the DC line, or very close, are used in a psychological way. Usually, it is to gain partners by controlling them or by giving in to them. Be aware that giving in is also a form of control. Planets here let others (the partners) do all the work and then pull the strings in the background. For example, Venus in Taurus on the DC wants both harmony and security in their closest relationships, so they will dismiss people who don't fit in with their perfect picture. But if someone provides either harmony or security, Venus in Taurus on the DC may begin a relationship with them and then manage their partner until they have their ideal relationship. If their partner is determined to avoid being moulded, the relationship will probably fail after a time. This is just one example of a planet on the DC. In effect, planets here *know what they want from relationships.*

MC planets want to control and take charge of a group. Inwardly, they feel perfectly capable of being in charge, and this confidence inspires others to believe in them. MC planets have a sense of destiny. *They know where they are going.* Thus, they expect to be admired and respected.

Obviously, the astrological sign the planet is in will colour the overall feel of the angle, but this is how angles work in principle. In the following sections, I will discuss overall keywords and themes for each planet on the angles. Remember, the planet has to be right on the line or within two degrees. Planets in other areas of the house are still important, but they are not quite as decisive and sure as they are when they are very close to the angle lines.

## Sun on the Angles

**AC:** Confident, unruffled, sure of themselves.

**IC:** Calm, sure, determined and with great staying power, but obstinate. A deep sense of personal honour and integrity.

**DC:** Won't allow others to get too close or personal unless their needs are met; then gains their sense of identity from their partner, so they become reliant and needy. An ability to use others for their own gain in a hidden way.

**MC:** Leadership, a sense of superiority, bossy, sure of their abilities, willing and able to take responsibility.

## Moon on the Angles

**AC:** A sympathetic listener with apparent empathy, but it may not be genuine.

**IC:** A preference for being alone. Sensitive but self-reliant.

**DC:** An innate ability to understand others' needs. Able to listen and sympathise. People are drawn to confide in them, so they make good counselors.

**MC:** In work settings, attuned to the group. Able to understand nuances and feelings. Possesses an outwardly calm understanding that encourages people to have confidence in them.

## Mercury on the Angles

AC: Chatty, lively, youthful. They say what they think people want to hear.

IC: Good powers of analysis. Emotionally guarded, but can make sound judgments.

DC: Open. Happy to discuss partnership matters. Willing to accept others' opinions.

MC: Good communicator with good ideas, often original. Great public speakers. Witty and clever.

## Venus on the Angles

AC: An easy manner, with the ability to sense the best way of handling people. Apparent warmth, but it is slightly deceptive.

IC: Strives to create a harmonious environment with those close to them; likes a pleasant home. Upset by aggression, harshness, or rudeness.

DC: Willing to go with others' ideas, but a bit naïve. Easily misled and deceived by others. They remain enthusiastic and optimistic even in the face of difficulties.

MC: Able to make work enjoyable. Finds it easy to bring people together in a joint enterprise.

## Mars on the Angles

AC: Blunt and argumentative. Says it exactly how it is, thus blithely treading on other people's toes. Sure of themselves and confrontational.

IC: Focused on their path. Determined and driven to be themselves and hold firm regardless of outside influences.

DC: Determined, strong-willed, unwilling to give an inch. In relationships with others, bossy and argumentative.

MC: Fearless, willing to try anything, led by gut instinct. Somehow, they always land on their feet.

# Jupiter on the Angles

**AC:** Goodwill toward others. Hopeful, generous, and able to inspire harmony.

**IC:** Good-natured, tolerant, and generous to those close to them.

**DC:** Cheerful, optimistic, and generous in relationships, maybe giving and expecting too much. Quite blunt.

**MC:** Undaunted, good-humoured, and able to shrug off problems. May give up on a career before fully trying it out; inclined to restlessness.

# Saturn on the Angles

**AC:** Poised, self-possessed, sure of their opinions but slightly reserved. Good analytical and critical facilities; able to quickly assess others.

**IC:** Unpretentious and modest. Hiding nothing but defending nothing. Non-judgmental and reserved.

**DC:** Calm and serious. Always ready to shoulder responsibilities and go the extra mile. Unadventurous and traditional in relationships.

**MC:** Does not like to be dependent and will keep their own space private. Prefers to work alone. Hard to get to know in a workplace. Expects a full day's work for a full day's pay.

# Uranus on the Angles

**AC:** Eccentric and original with a unique point of view. Enjoys shocking people with their clothing or their words. Needs personal space.

**IC:** Likes to make sudden, dramatic changes to their environment and lifestyle if things become too restricting. Doesn't feel tied by anything. A free spirit.

**DC:** Detached from relationships; everyone is a friend, even a lover or long-term partner. Enjoys being in partnerships as long as they don't impinge on their freedom.

**MC:** A visionary with idealistic aims. Recognises no authority but their own. Perceptive and quick to spot scams. Won't conform.

# Neptune on the Angles

**AC:** Receptive to others and senses emotional undercurrents. Easily misled.

**IC:** Idealistic, hopeful, and trusting.

**DC:** Pleasant and trusting of others, thus inclined to be easily deceived in relationships. Needs no personal reassurance from others. A bit detached and emotionally cool.

**MC:** Lack of worldly ambition means they go through the motions but rarely feel driven to achieve material success. In truth, they prefer to be left alone.

# Pluto on the Angles

**AC:** They make a strong first impression. People instinctively know this is a person who knows who they are and can't be manipulated. Always on the lookout for an opportunity (business or romantic).

**IC:** Stubborn, though they appear outwardly accepting. Adept at using guile and psychology to get people to do what they want.

**DC:** Controlling, hard to please, and very aware of other people's attempts at control and manipulation, as they are masters at this. Seeks someone they can rule.

**MC:** Confident, decisive, capable, sure of themselves. Happy to be in charge—in fact, they demand it. Will leave no stone unturned to make a business a success and is always on the lookout for a new angle or subtle way to outmanoeuvre the competition.

# Rulers on Angles

Now let's take a quick look at how it affects a birth chart when any of the angles have their astrological ruler in that house. The ruler is the planet that "rules" that astrological sign. Remember, the angles are the AC, IC, DC, and MC. When the line that denotes these has its astrological ruler right on or within a few degrees of it, this perfect matching of a sign and its ruler gives people an even greater self-confidence in the area it appears.

Here is a reminder of which planet rules which sign: Mars rules the sign of Aries, Venus rules the sign of Taurus, Mercury rules the sign of Gemini, the moon rules the sign of Cancer, the sun rules the sign of Leo, Mercury rules the sign of Virgo, Venus rules the sign of Libra, Pluto rules the sign of Scorpio, Jupiter rules the sign of Sagittarius, Saturn rules the sign of Capricorn, Uranus rules the sign of Aquarius, and Neptune rules the sign of Pisces.

So, have a look at your chart. Which astrological sign is your AC (and first house)? Which planet rules that astrological sign? Reference the previous paragraph. For example, if your AC and first house is Aries, it is ruled by Mars. Is Mars on the actual AC line or within two degrees of it? If it is, look below at AC ruler on AC to see what it means. If Mars isn't in Aries, then it doesn't apply. But go on and check your other angles. Which astrological sign is your IC line starting? If the sign is Capricorn, Saturn rules it, and if Saturn is right on the IC line or within two degrees of it, check below to see what it means. Do this with the other two angles as well.

If you have no planets on any of the angles (or within two degrees of these lines), you can disregard this section, as it only applies when the planet that rules that sign is present.

**AC Ruler on AC:** Self-possessed, straightforward, direct, they are able to be themselves with no subterfuge.

**DC Ruler on DC:** Confident, positive, self-reliant. They don't need others to feel complete, so they attract others that dislike being leant on.

**IC Ruler on IC:** Friendly and sociable. Underneath, they are loners, preferring to live and work alone.

**MC ruler on MC:** Able to make the best of any situation, with complete faith in themselves.

☽ ✳ ☾

This information regarding rulers and angles is often overlooked in charts, but from my experience it is a valuable tool in understanding both ourselves and others. If you see a chart that has planets on any of the angles, it is worth checking to see how it affects that person. Confident, quietly assured people often have these—and this is especially relevant if the planet is a ruler of that sign. This is an accurate guide to some quite subtle nuances in a chart, and if you have one or more planets on angles yourself, you will certainly be able to relate to the information in this chapter.

*Nine*
# NORTH AND SOUTH NODES

The north nodes are now generally thought to be our karmic destiny, the path a person must follow in life to find true happiness and fulfilment. In ancient times the nodes were not even considered as part of our birth charts, but like Saturn, the more we have grown spiritually, the more astrologers have continued to discover. The north node is actually a mathematical point related to the positions of the sun, moon, and Earth at an individual's moment of birth. In exact (but sometimes confusing terms), the north node is the point at which the moon's orbit intersected the plane of the ecliptic. That is the technical description, but you only need to remember that this point has long been considered karmic.

The south node, which is not marked on a birth chart but is exactly opposite the north node, is considered the area (by astrological sign and house) that we have fully experienced in the last life. It is a place we feel comfortable in, having had so many dealings with it previously. It is our "comfort zone."

This theory of the nodes does indicate a past existence of some form or another. And whatever you choose to believe, the nodes are certainly an important tool when analysing someone's birth chart, especially when doing a full chart interpretation. In most cases, a chart will have planetary placements that, when analysed, are all pointing in the same direction, with the north and south nodes often serving as a final confirmation of what has already been discovered.

Despite many astrologers theorizing that following the north node position brings happiness and fulfilment, my belief is that few people willingly inhabit their north node house. This area is totally alien to them, making it unappealing, and they certainly do prefer the south node position. But it is true that life continually puts them in the north node house, so they are forced to deal with it in some way. Rather than the north node being an area of happiness, it appears to be something we all must grapple with.

My personal experience in the forty years or so that I have been interpreting charts is that those whose circumstances force them to live most of their lives in the north node house feel out of sync with it; it feels wrong somehow. They long for the comfort area of the opposite house. Always, there is a clinging to the south node house, and people go straight back to it as soon as the opportunity arises. At the very best, people who do live in their north node house form a reluctant acceptance rather than finding happiness or any sort of fulfilment. Because each house has many themes, it is usually the case that only one aspect of the north node house is actively adopted, the rest avoided.

There is an exception to this feeling of reluctance; those who have one or more planets in their north node house will have less difficulty confronting this life issue. A planet in a house draws us there, remember? Perhaps this situation helps them accept their north node house when they have failed in previous lives? This is conjecture, and you must form your own ideas and opinions as you study more charts. Spiritual beliefs and ideas are simply that, and it is up to the individual to draw their own conclusions.

Pull up your birth chart and look for the north node. It should be easy to find; the symbol for the north node looks like an earphone headset. Take note of its placement, both by house and astrological sign. The south node is unmarked, but it is exactly across from the north node in a birth chart. For example, if you have a Libra north node in the sixth house, your south node would be in Aries in the twelfth house. If determining the south node without a symbol is challenging, you can locate the south node by drawing a straight line from the north node to the exact opposite side of the chart, essentially cutting the chart in half. That position is the (unmarked) location of the south node.

First we will discuss north and south nodes by their house placement, which determines what an individual's karmic destiny is. Later in the chapter we will discuss north and south nodes by their astrological sign, which hints at how a person can achieve this destiny. Working off the previous example, if a birth chart has a Libra north node in the sixth house, you would read the section titled "North Node in Sixth House (South Node Twelfth House)" first and then the section titled "North Node in Libra (South Node in Aries)."

## North Node in First House (South Node in Seventh House)

This position has to do with relationships because the first house is the ascendant, ruled by Aries, and the south node is in the seventh house, the house of partnerships, which is ruled by Libra, the sign of compromise and balance. Therefore, this position is about being independent (first house/Aries) versus being dependent (seventh house/Libra).

The north node in the first house indicates that in a past life, this person would have had a long-term relationship or marriage where they totally relied on their partner. They deferred to their partner, compromised, and shared with them. Therefore, they have a natural ability to easily form lasting relationships. Consequently, they feel lost without a partner. They will usually marry or make a commitment very early in life, which means they may choose unsuitable partners simply because of their need to be with someone.

Because they submerged their whole personality to serve their partner before, they are now being asked to go to the first house and explore who they are as an individual, to begin to think of only themselves and to become more independent. To this end, it is actually fine for them to live alone. Marriage isn't necessary. In fact, it may even hinder their growth. They've proven they can do relationships, and now they have to find out how to manage things alone.

One way or another, they will be asked to analyse their personal dependence on others throughout their life. This may happen through losing a partner (either through divorce or death) or failed relationships, which will force them to try and do things on their own, even though it's likely they will immediately seek out another partner. Alternatively, they may have a partner who travels for work a lot of the time or a partner who becomes ill, forcing the individual to be more independent.

There are any number of ways this first/seventh balance may work itself out over an individual's life, but their focus will primarily be on personal relationships. This placement indicates that a person needs to learn to cope on their own and to rely on their own inner resources.

## North Node in Second House (South Node in Eighth House)

This position is all about money—their own in the second house (ruled by Taurus) versus other people's money in eighth house (ruled by Scorpio).

The south node in the eighth house means that in a past life these individuals relied on other people to provide for their needs. Because the eighth house is on the "others" side of the chart, it is probable that they totally relied on another person—sexually, emotionally, and financially. This south node placement feels comfortable and normal, so as soon as they are old enough to form relationships, they will unconsciously seek someone to share their life with who will continue this past life pattern.

In this lifetime, however, they are being asked to take responsibility for themselves. The north node in the second house advises them to learn to look after themselves (in financial terms especially) because the second house is all about personal finances and possessions. Their lessons in life will revolve around learning to stand on their own two feet and to work hard to secure their own position in the world without relying on anyone else.

This could manifest in many ways. It could be that a partner who looked after them is suddenly unable to do so and the individual is thrown back on their own resources, or perhaps a partner's money is lost in one way or another. This is the point when the individual will be required to step forward and develop their own talents and abilities through hard work and dedication. It will be tempting to relax back into being taken care of, but time and again the rug will be pulled out from under them. Gradually, they will learn to be more self-sufficient and to value their own talents.

## North Node in Third House (South Node in Ninth House)

This node position is all about education, learning, and teaching. Communication, in effect.

The south node is in the ninth house of wisdom and esoteric thought. It is above the AC/DC line and in the individual thinking quadrant. This indicates that their past life would have been spent alone thinking, travelling, researching, theorising, and thus enabling the individual to come up with their own theories about the meaning of life. They come into this life with an esoteric knowledge beyond their years; they carry a certain benign surety in their beliefs. But there is a sense of separateness from other people due to the fact that they spent so much time alone in a past life.

The third house is ruled by Gemini, the sign of communication, and it is down in the collective community part of a birth chart. So, with the north node in the third house, this person is being called on to mix with everyone—friends, family, and neighbours—in this life. Having learnt so much last time, they now have to pass on their knowledge.

People with their north node in the third house are messengers, bringers of wisdom and advice, and they have to find ways to impart their knowledge in a way ordinary people can understand and relate to. They have to present their facts in a simple and unambiguous way; each time they get too flowery or intellectual, they will be reminded that their audience is unable to understand what they are trying to say. They must hone and polish their skills to present things in a way everyone can understand.

These individuals always want to escape back to their ivory tower, to the peaceful ninth house, but life will present opportunities for them to teach what they know. They will always be encouraged down into the third house, and their hard work will be rewarded by the joy they feel when exchanging information.

## North Node in Fourth House (South Node in Tenth House)

This node position is all about the balance between the home (fourth house) and the career (tenth house).

In a past life, all of this person's lessons were about the tenth house, the house of career. The tenth house is ruled by Capricorn and is very traditional. It is likely that this person spent their past life climbing the career ladder. Because of this, they feel comfortable being in control and managing others, and they enjoy being respected and admired for their business acumen. They came into this life with a natural understanding of the commercial and business world, so it is easy for them to rise to the top of their profession.

However, the individual has proven their expertise in this area already. Now, in this life, they have to learn all about the fourth house of home and family. They must drop to the bottom of the chart and serve willingly and without recognition, except from their family. Instead of business relationships, they are being asked to experience emotional relationships.

It is comfortable for this individual to seek recognition and praise, but this is unlikely in the home, where work is often tedious and unsung; many people work long and hard for their families and rarely get recognition. Without this praise, they feel unvalued and struggle with feelings of inadequacy. Yet the more they try to show themselves to others in a good light, the more frustrated they will feel, as this is not what others want. Others want this person to serve the family—to cook and garden, to create a harmonious and peaceful home life, and to support them.

It will be hard for this person to release this need for recognition and to learn to sublimate their talents in service to their family, but their family will benefit from their knowledge in many ways as they guide and advise from this more mundane level. Their only praise will be from family, but this individual will come to appreciate that familial praise is more valuable and rewarding than praise from the wider world. Their task is to let go of the desire to rule and learn to selflessly serve.

## North Node in Fifth House (South Node in Eleventh House)

These two houses are all about interaction with others.

The south node is in the eleventh house. This is a place where groups of enlightened and intelligent people make decisions on behalf of others. Because the eleventh house is at the top of the chart and above the collective community, this person probably had a high-profile career in a previous life. They likely mixed with philosophers, philanthropists, and people of consequence in positions of authority. This is a comfortable place for them, and as soon as they are able, they will be pulled toward joining groups and societies that reflect their talents and interests. There is no doubt that they are intellectual and farseeing, and they want to use their talents to make a difference to other people's lives as they did in the last life—but they prefer to be removed from direct contact.

In this lifetime, though, they are being asked to come down into the collective community and to mix with all sorts of people in the bawdy fifth house. Imagine a bar or club full of rowdy, lively people and you see the opposite extreme of the eleventh house and its rarefied atmosphere. The eleventh house is ruled by Aquarius, which is detached from emotions, but now this individual must strive to form one-on-one personal relationships in the house ruled by Leo.

Life will connect the two houses in a way that forces this person to spend more time rubbing shoulders with people from all walks of life, perhaps through their career. As the fifth house is the house of creativity, many people with fifth house north nodes find that by becoming artists, writers, musicians, or actors, they naturally become closely involved with others. Doctors, medical specialists, and healthcare workers also need strong links to the fifth house. Any talent that involves direct contact with ordinary people is helping bring the individual down to their north node position.

The fifth house is a place of creativity and self-expression, so this person will be learning how to express their unique individuality rather than expressing it collectively as a group. Another way to do this is through having children and experiencing love affairs; any direct, one-on-one physical contact is their task. Their lessons are about connecting themselves to the basic creativity of life.

## North Node in Sixth House (South Node in Twelfth House)

These nodes are about physical work (sixth) against reflective meditation (twelfth).

The sixth house is all about service to others. It involves practical physical work and implies a literal rolling up of one's sleeves. This sort of work is below the AC/DC line. Since it is in the community section of the birth chart, the work is usually unseen and unsung.

This will be a hard task for those from the twelfth house south node position. Not because they are lazy, but because they spent their past life in retreat, far away from the world's busy activity, watching the world but not being part of it. This person would have spent a lot of time alone in quiet contemplation, so they had the leisure and peace to develop their own spiritual ideals. The beliefs they formed during that lifetime of quiet contemplation now have to be put into practice in the sixth house of service. To do this, they must actively pursue situations that require real labour in a caring capacity.

As with all node positions, there will always be the call to retreat back to what they are familiar with. Time and again, life will present situations where the individual can fulfil their sixth house role, and time and again they will draw back from it. Like all positions that are above the AC/DC line, they feel removed from the hubbub of life; they fear diving into community situations. This person enjoys their own company and peace and quiet.

With this position, there are often other pointers that will help them follow the right path, such as a sun in the bottom part of the chart or another planet in the sixth house. These nodes are telling them they have to strive to do physical, hands-on labour willingly and humbly to really live the ideals they formed in the last life.

## North Node in Seventh House (South Node in First House)

This is the relationship axis, so this node position is about how the individual relates to others.

This person's last life dealt with the concerns of the first house, the ascendant, on the "me" side of the chart. Because the south node is here, these individuals learned how to be independent of others. They probably lived alone or were very detached from relationships, and they managed just fine without a committed partnership. But the seventh house is about long-term, one-on-one relationships and marriage. It is about compromise and balance and taking the needs of another into account.

This is the individual's challenge: to learn that no person is an island and that they really do need others. Putting another's needs before their own will be a constant challenge, and they may avoid any sort of commitment for a long while, or they may avoid any partnership that they see as threatening to their identity. By committing to a relationship, they feel they are signing away a part of themselves.

Even if they do finally make a commitment, their partners may complain that they are selfish or detached. Their task is to find a way to overcome this fear of leaning into another. They must let go of their own autonomy and of being reliant on someone else. Life will teach them how to compromise and share—perhaps through failed relationships, because of this inability to give wholly of themselves. As they age, they will assess the way they relate. Gradually, this person will learn how to be fully committed to another.

## North Node in Eighth House (South Node in Second House)

This node position is all about money—the individual's (second house) and other people's (eighth house).

In a past life, these people would have focused all their efforts on second house issues. They managed to create a safe, secure environment for themselves and their loved ones by working hard and saving money. It is likely that they accumulated wealth and property because the second house is ruled by Taurus, so the individual sought safety and security through money and possessions. In this lifetime, it will be very tempting to follow this same pattern of being self-reliant and looking after others because it will come naturally to them.

But the north node in the eighth house means that in this lifetime, the individual has to learn to rely on others. Life usually presents situations that allow this to happen, and it may be that for some reason they can't support themselves. This might happen through redundancy, for health reasons, or simply because their time is committed elsewhere. This reliance on others won't happen immediately, but over the course of the individual's life, their attitude will shift and change in imperceptible ways, gradually bringing them to the opposite of what they are used to.

It won't be easy for them to hand over control to others. It is comfortable for them to be in charge of their own finances and make their own decisions. Their challenge in this life is to learn how to graciously accept help from others and to allow others to take charge of this area. This person has to learn how to *take* when they have been accustomed to *give*.

## North Node in Ninth House (South Node in Third House)

This node position is about learning, teaching, and communicating knowledge.

The south node's position in the third house indicates that in a past life, these individuals believed, without question, what their teachers and others in authority told them. This level of learning is available within the collective community, so it would be school level. A great many people with the south node in the third house are teachers and educators of school-age children because they are good at what they do, having spent a previous lifetime honing their skills. They are comfortable in the collective and enjoy contributing to their local community, making many friendships and keeping a busy schedule.

To get to their north node in the ninth house involves study at a higher level, at university and beyond. But the last thing this person wants to do is head up to the ninth house and study subjects in-depth or come up with their own opinions and ideas. It feels safe following the rules of what to teach and how and when. The north node in the ninth house also requires them to be alone because the ninth house involves private, personal study, the search for their own meaning in life, and the quest for a higher truth. This is something that does not appeal to this person in the least.

With this node position, they are being asked to move away from collective thinking and to seek their own answers to the big questions of life. This person doesn't feel equipped to do this at all, and they are anxious about expressing anything other than accepted, traditional beliefs, yet in one way or another they will find a way to learn things for themselves. And, much to their surprise, people will listen to and value their opinions. Life will present opportunities to expand their knowledge beyond mere rote, and this person should grasp any chance to learn subjects beyond the usual scope. This is an esoteric house, so the individual may find that they have spiritual or psychic gifts hidden away inside, and they should strive to bring these hidden talents forward.

## North Node in Tenth House (South Node in Fourth House)

These nodes are concerned with the axis between the home (fourth house) and the career (tenth house).

This individual spent their previous life in the fourth house of home and family and devoted all their time and attention to them; everything they did was motivated by that love. They come into this life with a natural ability and talent to create a loving and caring home for others and probably start out in adult life doing just that. They will enjoy creating a nurturing environment, doing all those jobs in a household that show caring: cooking, cleaning, gardening, or supporting everyone as best they can. People with this position often choose partners or loved ones who are in need of special care.

But this time around, this person has to go up to the tenth house, to find their way in the commercial, business world. With this north node position, a career is the way they can do this. Life will present many opportunities for them to make this change, often very gradually. It may be that for a while they may voluntarily (or otherwise) have to separate from their childhood family, to leave behind that emotional and financial support. It will feel scary, but somewhere along the way they will come to realise that the goals set by their birth family are not the right ones for them, that they are actually out of sync with their own family's beliefs, and that they have to forge their own path in life.

As they grow in maturity and confidence in their own abilities beyond the familial environment, they will be able to reestablish their roots and links to their family on a different—and better—footing. There will always be a deep bond with their family, even if they are separated. This person may seek to balance their life by creating another family of their own, but each time they endeavour to create that family unit, they eventually realise they are not in tune with them. Thus, life gradually presents a way of showing them how to leave emotional relationships behind to create commercial, business links instead. Many of these people go on to create a family feeling within a business, thus linking the two node positions.

This does not mean someone with a north node in the tenth house cannot have a family of their own, but it must be one in which they are supported and cared for, not the other way around. Any attempt to be the carer will not work. They are destined to forge their own career, one that brings responsibility, status, and acclaim; this is their destiny. The most obvious result of this fourth/tenth house axis is working from home, where the individual can combine the two aspects: their love of family and their path to career success—but they must allow others to do the caring and focus on their career.

# North Node in Eleventh House (South Node in Fifth House)

This node position is all about interactions with others.

When the south node is in the fifth house, it indicates that in a past life this person happily mixed with everyone and anyone, and they would have had a lot of close contact with people from all walks of life. They might have had random love affairs or children by different partners, all of which taught them about human relationships. They come into this life with a natural ability and desire to recreate these same behaviour patterns. The south node is down in the collective area of busy activity, and this is where they feel comfortable: in bars and clubs, in groups of friends and family, and deep in the middle of community affairs.

With the north node in the Aquarian eleventh house, this person has to learn to detach themselves from close human relationships and be more discerning in whom they choose to mix with during this lifetime. The eleventh house is more about friendship than love; it is a place detached from deeply emotional feelings. The eleventh house is concerned with intellectual decisions. Basically, it is more important to be friends rather than lovers.

To achieve this, this person has to learn to resist accepting every romantic opportunity. They are being asked to move up to the top of the chart, to be detached and humanitarian rather than personally involved. It is enormously valuable to have this knowledge and experience of the fifth house because they can make decisions about the best way to help those in the collective community, and this is what being in the eleventh house is about: improving the lives of others through groups and associations while using their acquired knowledge and insight.

As with all node positions, this doesn't happen overnight. It occurs over a lifetime of gradual shifts and changes. One way or another, the individual's attitude will change and they will start to draw back from the drama of the fifth house—from the need be at the centre of attention. This person will no longer feel the need to dance on a table and party the night away; no longer will they seek liaisons of all kinds with people from all walks of life.

The eleventh house is peopled by intellectuals. It is up in the actions for others quadrant, so this person's natural abilities will gradually lift them to a higher part of the chart. Their talents will force them to mix with people from the eleventh house. They will be required to join groups and societies whose aims are humanitarian, forcing them to realize that they can better help those in the collective community through their talents rather than by being at the hub of everything.

## North Node in Twelfth House (South Node in Sixth House)

These nodes are about reflective meditation (twelfth house) rather than physical work and caring (sixth house).

If the south node is in the sixth house, the house of service, this individual would have willingly done things to help others in practical, hands-on ways in a past life. People with these nodes are very hardworking and never shirk an opportunity to offer their assistance for any task. Sensing this, others will ask this person to help out time and again, and they are willing to do so. It will be hard for them to say no because working hard is second nature to them.

But in this lifetime, they are being asked to stand back, to go to the twelfth house of spiritual enlightenment in the actions for others quadrant. They are meant to retire from life and meditate. This time they only have to *be*. It will be hard for them to stop working because it means a reliance on others—of taking instead of giving, and giving is second nature to them. Leaning on others means giving up their personal autonomy, which will be hard. Moving from the sixth house to the twelfth house means moving from a physically active life to a quiet, contemplative life. It means being less active and more spiritually aware.

If the individual doesn't say no to hard work and other people's constant demands, life will create situations that make it impossible for them to repeat their past life pattern. One way or another, they will be forced into the twelfth house. Sometimes illness forces them to retreat and retire because they are then no longer able to undertake physical responsibilities or work long hours.

Often, these shifts are made over a whole lifetime, so it will be a gradual process. But, as with all node positions, if this person doesn't take conscious steps toward their north node, life will pull the rug out from under them in some way or another. There will always be a need for a productive, active life, but a balance must be found so that they have long, quiet reflection time to think about the meaning of life itself.

☽ ✴ ☾

Now we come to the astrological sign the north node is in. This position gives a more detailed picture of exactly how the life lessons can be learned.

## North Node in Aries (South Node in Libra)

Coming from the sign of Libra—which deals with partnerships—means this person will see all sides of issues, making it almost impossible for them to come to any decisions. They think that what other people want is what they want. Keeping the peace and compromising is second nature to them. It is a well-known fact that you can't please everyone all of the time, yet they will attempt to do so, exhausting themselves trying to make everyone happy.

In this lifetime, with their north node in Aries, this individual has to learn to think about themselves. An Aries puts themselves first, so they will be encouraged to stop prioritizing others and to make their own decisions. They will be forced, one way or another, to assume a more independent role in this life.

Their thought processes will be less balanced and logical (Libra) and more instinctive (Aries). They need to learn to take action immediately, relying on their gut feeling instead of going by what others think. They must learn not to spend too long considering how their decisions will affect others. As with all node positions, life will provide opportunities for these lessons to be learned, so there will be a point where they will be forced to act. They should take charge whenever they can. Their Libra south node has made them passive, compromising, and afraid of being alone; this life's lessons are teaching them the exact opposite.

## North Node in Taurus (South Node in Scorpio)

Scorpio is a deeply emotional, passionate, and suspicious sign, so people with this south node are always creating dramatic situations. They are renowned for destroying good relationships because of their desire to stir up things up based on jealousy, suspicion, or just plain boredom. They deliberately upset the peace by creating emotional drama, then blame the result on others. This does not make for happy relationships or peaceful unions.

In this lifetime, this person has to learn to control those emotions and to be more Taurean. They have to accept that it is okay to just *be,* that others are genuine, and that not all people have hidden motives. They must learn to see the best in people rather than assume the worst and to stop rocking the partnership boat just because they like life to be dramatic.

In this lifetime, they will learn to accept others as they are. They will also learn how to live a quiet, mundane existence in peace and harmony. It will teach them to be responsible for themselves financially (Taurus rules the second house). It helps if they learn to appreciate the arts and the nature—anything that soothes those passionate emotions. This person should go for long walks, paint, or take up an instrument; art brings solace, and Taurus likes green spaces.

## North Node in Gemini (South Node in Sagittarius)

Coming from the sign of Sagittarius, these people have so much wisdom from their last life that they now find it hard to relate to people on an ordinary level. They feel out of step with society, often eschewing the ordinary rituals of traditional life like weddings and funerals, as well as anything that is expected of them that they believe has no meaningful basis. But, despite feeling this way, verbalising and confessing to it is quite hard for them. Maybe they understand why others find comfort in tradition and don't wish to destroy their contentment?

This person cannot help needing to be different or refusing to conform to what people expect. Yet, in this life, they are destined to relate to others, to accept those traditions that are necessary when people live cheek by jowl. For example, they may have to live with others in the collective community whereas they lived alone in a past life. Because of this—and against their own inner feelings—they will come to accept society's rules, manners, and customs. This person will find themselves in positions where they must make small talk, be polite, and accept social norms. Gradually, it will occur to them that everyone is in a mutually beneficial relationship and that everyone relies on each other; society only works if the majority follow the rules.

## North Node in Cancer (South Node in Capricorn)

The south node in Capricorn endows this person with expertise when it comes to being in charge of others, running a business, or forging a career that brings status and rewards. Respect and recognition are important to them.

In this lifetime, they still need and expect recognition, but no matter how much they try, their efforts will never quite succeed. This is because they are not being asked to assume a position of leadership this time; they are being asked to look after their family. They have to learn to be more humble, to be one of many rather than an individual, and to take their place in the family group. Trouble comes when they try to lead and control others or when they overwork themselves in desperation for recognition, which never comes.

This individual has to learn to let the world go by without actively taking part, to concentrate on the needs of those closest to them, to be more Cancerian: to be more caring in a personal way, to serve those they love without any thanks.

## North Node in Leo (South Node in Aquarius)

Aquarius is the sign of many friendships. It is also nonjudgmental. Therefore, in their last life, these people were cool and detached in personal matters; it is unlikely they were materialistic or had a large ego.

In this lifetime, this person is being called on to be more personal, more Leo-like. They must force themselves to be centre stage; it is no good being detached and impersonal or watching the world from a distance. They are being asked to involve themselves with everyone and to come into close contact with all sorts of people.

Aquarius and Leo have something in common: the need to be of service to humanity. But Aquarius does this unsung, and Leo does it in a blaze of glory. It is time to shine in the limelight. To do this, this person will need to overcome their innate shyness. They will need to be bold, taking an idea and running with it. They should take any leadership positions offered to them. Even though this person believes everyone is equal, they must learn that some are better at leading than others. This lifetime will show them how.

## North Node in Virgo (South Node in Pisces)

Pisces creates individuals with great compassion and understanding. Not worldly and always taking the line of least resistance, it is unlikely this person had any material or financial success in a past life. They likely suffered from a lack of confidence and an inability to make logical decisions. This person comes into this life still carrying their capacity to be long-suffering and with the ability to easily empathise with others. In this lifetime, they must learn to stop taking on the burdens of others. It is important to discriminate between those they really can help and those who will be a drain on them.

This position is all about serving others. While in Pisces, this person served everyone without any discrimination. Now they must serve only those who really need it. They cannot carry everyone who leans on them. Virgos still serves others, but they do it more practically. A Virgo attends to details and organises; they work hard. So, in this lifetime, it is through physical work that this person will find their true self. They have to stop daydreaming and start taking action. They must avoid the desire to retreat back to a chaotic, dreamy existence and remain focused on practical jobs. They have to overcome that old habit of overlooking and forgiving unacceptable behaviour. They need to learn to draw the line between those they can help and those they can't.

## North Node in Libra (South Node in Aries)

Coming from the sign of Aries means these people are courageous, impulsive action-takers. They are self-centred but full of confidence and vitality, ready to do anything or go anywhere at the drop of a hat. This is all fine, as far as their last life went. They were supposed to be strong; they were meant to be physically bold. Now, though, they are being asked to follow the opposite path. This lifetime is all about learning to compromise and share. They must focus on the needs of others, which they must balance with their own desires in order to move from Aries qualities to Libra qualities.

It is through partnerships that this person's best lessons come because in a partnership, they can learn to put someone else's needs before their own. This person has to stop and think before taking action; they need to remember to ask the opinions of their partners. In this lifetime, they must learn to cooperate and compromise.

## North Node in Scorpio (South Node in Taurus)

The sign of Taurus is fixed earth. Like the bull it represents, these individuals come into this life with strength, determination, and absolutely fixed ideas. They also have the ability to work hard and accumulate wealth through their own efforts; their possessions bring them a sense of security.

In this lifetime, they are being asked to experience life through the sign of Scorpio. Scorpio opens the door to emotions and feelings they have not experienced—to passions that are not always physical. The security they so need may be taken from them, so instead of providing for others, they may find they have to rely on others instead. This person finds it easy to give, but now they have to learn how to receive and how to feel more deeply. This lifetime's lesson is what it is like to be dependent on someone else.

## North Node in Sagittarius (South Node in Gemini)

Gemini is mutable air. This is how they would have presented themselves in their last life: saying what they thought people wanted them to say, believing nothing in particular except what was expedient at the time. They had many friends, even more acquaintances, and disliked anything that called for commitment on their part. Relationships would have been abandoned as soon as they impinged on their freedom.

Now, this person has to move to a higher level. The sign of Sagittarius is that of esoteric thought. In this life, they will be forced to look more deeply at the meaning of existence. One way or another, they will be isolated from the world at various times so that they are forced to spend time thinking for themselves. Accepting what other people think just to please them no longer works—in this lifetime, they have to find their own answers to the big questions.

## North Node in Capricorn (South Node in Cancer)

Coming from the sign of Cancer means that in a past life, this person looked after people, most likely their own family. They are nurturing and caring, always willing to do things for other people. They feel comfortable in the home or caring for others.

However, in this lifetime they have to find a way to express themselves through their career. This will not be easy because in their early life, they will not feel ambitious or even interested in the outside world; their family is everything to them. Gradually, they will realise that their family does not need them—that they are not as important to their family as they thought. But there will be a freedom in not having to be all things to all people, leaving this person time to find a way to express their own identity through their career. Because their north node is in the sign of Capricorn, whose ruler is Saturn, this career often comes later in life after many setbacks.

## North Node in Aquarius (South Node in Leo)

Leo is the sign of royalty, so these people still carry within them the feeling that they are special. In a past life, they were definitely the centre of someone's universe and in a leadership role that called for others' admiration and praise. It will be hard to throw off this attitude. This person has an innate feeling that they are better than everyone else, so they will only mix with people they perceive to be their social equals or higher—those who stroke their ego and remind them of how wonderful they are.

In this lifetime, Aquarius is calling for this person to start seeing the world as a mixture of equals, to be more detached and put friendship before love, and to be less ego-driven. Paths will appear that encourage them to use their life for a higher purpose, for furthering humanitarian aims. Putting the group first is the only real way to fulfilment, and any personal rewards this person achieves in this lifetime will feel hollow unless accompanied by the gesture and actions of a humanitarian.

## North Node in Pisces (South Node in Virgo)

The longer these people live, the more they will realise how rigid and judgmental they are; their past life in Virgo endowed them with a need for structure, rules, and regulations. The world, though, is a disorganised place. Trying to tidy everything, organise people, and bring structure where there is none will exhaust them, perhaps even making them ill. They become irritable when people continue to go their own way despite this person's very best attempts to bring everything into alignment.

The key to happiness is for this person to learn to go with the flow. They need to stop trying to be in control, instead letting things and people be. The world will not fall apart if this person is not there to pick up the pieces. In other words, they should stop thinking and start feeling. Pisces has nothing to do with logic or reason and everything to do with instinct and intuition. This person needs to learn to stand back and let life go on—to accept that it is what it is, and they are not responsible for anyone anymore.

☽ ✳ ☾

Can you relate to what your nodes are saying? They certainly are a powerful tool for finding out what we should be doing in life, and for acknowledging where we feel most at home.

Check out the charts of your friends and family and see if they have a similar comfortable feeling for their south node house and a reluctance for the north node house. It is usually uncanny how accurate they are!

## Ten
# THE FAMILY MODEL

*F*or this chapter, thanks must go to Bruno and Louise Huber. Swiss psychologists and astrologers, they developed a modern psychological method of interpreting charts and opened Huber schools in Europe during the 1970s and '80s to teach their particular approach. This lesson was learnt directly through them, and it has been so incredibly accurate that no alterations or changes have ever been necessary; it works.

It is quite easy to look at a birth chart and see how someone fared in childhood based on what the Hubers called the Family Model. At a glance, how an individual perceives their mother and father and their own position within the family unit becomes apparent.

Every child in a family will regard their own position differently. Siblings often have contrasting ideas about their parents and their parents' expectations of them, dependent on where the sun, Saturn, and moon appear in their chart. This can be attributed to having their own chart, which will give them their own unique personality. Thus, siblings see or perceive their parents and their position within the family unit in a different light. Yet all siblings in the same family will still clearly see similarities in their parents' behaviour even if they have no knowledge of astrology.

Before we begin, I want to mention that it isn't strictly necessary to know about the family model when interpreting a chart, but it does provide greater depth, especially as many problems in adulthood stem from childhood difficulties and traumas.

So, let's look at the Family Model. In a birth chart, the sun represents the individual's father (or father figure). Saturn represents the mother (or mother figure) because she is usually the one who instils the rules and regulations in a household and, in most cases, holds the family unit together. The moon is the individual as a child. These positions in a birth chart provide a good indication of how the individual viewed their family as a child and where they perceived they stood in relation to their parents.

## The Sun (The Father or Father Figure)

The position of the sun in a birth chart indicates whether an individual saw their father as a good father—if he was seen as setting a good example. For this we look to see what house the sun is in. The ideal position of the sun in someone's chart is between the eighth and eleventh houses, which is indicative of a positive relationship with their father.

If the sun is on or close to the AC (ascendant), or anywhere in the twelfth or first house, the father appeared too reserved to get to know well. Perhaps he spent a lot of time in his study or office, or maybe he was just a very reserved person, unable to share his thoughts and feelings with his child.

The sun right on the DC (descendant), close to it, or in the seventh house means the child most likely viewed their father as being too involved with other people. He would have been out and about with others most of the time, whether at work or socialising with friends, instead of focusing on his child.

Either way, whether the sun is in the AC or the DC houses, the child will be left with a feeling of being unloved. The father was secluded on his own or out with others rather than being with his child.

If the sun is low in a birth chart (in houses one through six), the child thought their father failed them in some way. Ideally, the sun would be high in the chart so that the child can look up to their father. If the sun is on the MC (midheaven) or in the tenth house, the father is suitably high in the chart, but he might have been too involved in his career to be a perfect father. This is still a positive position for the sun overall. The child can accept that absence, because in most societies, fathers are expected to be out working.

In an individual's birth chart, their sun's astrological sign is a reflection of how they viewed their father during childhood. People display the energy of their astrological sign quite clearly, even when there is no knowledge of astrology. So, if the child's sun is in a fire sign, their father likely appeared masculine, aggressive, argumentative, or busy. An air sign father (sun) might have appeared a little detached from family relationships, but he would have been able to talk about many subjects with his child, or he would have been technically clever and able to help them with that side of life. An earth sign father was a sensible, hands-on chap, maybe encouraging the child to under-take practical activities with him or to accompany him on activities in the outdoors. A water sign father was a compassionate, understanding person, someone the child could confide in without fear of shame or ridicule. The exception is if the child's sun sign is in Scorpio, in which case the child prob-ably found their father difficult to fathom.

Look carefully at the exact position of the sun. If it is in an astrological sign that does not have a house cusp (intercepted), the sun has no access to an area of life. Thus, the father was seen as someone weak, someone who was given orders by his partner, or someone who appeared ineffective. Just like everyone else, the child cannot see who their father truly is because the sun cannot function properly in the outside world. This likely caused problems for the father, too; specifically, the knowledge that people did not understand him—a difficult situation for all involved.

Any planet conjunct the sun will colour the child's view of their father, depending on the planet. For example, if Mercury is conjunct the sun, the child may have felt that their father always hid behind a newspaper or was often engaging with others in conversation. If Mars is conjunct the sun, the father was perceived as forceful and aggressive—in other words, more like a fire sign sun. This combination of planets works just like any other conjunc-tion, and children pick up on the nuances very quickly.

## Saturn (The Mother or Mother Figure)

Saturn is regarded as the mother, as the mother figure traditionally provides the physical comforts, necessities, rules, and regulations in the household.

Obviously, there are variations on this, but in general, this is the mother's role as a child grows into adulthood.

The ideal position for Saturn is at the bottom of the chart (houses two through five). If Saturn is here, the child's connection to their mother feels secure and they are better able to face life's problems. These houses are part of the collective community, and the child needs the security of knowing their mother is at home (or in the local community) and that she will take them to school, help them find friends and work, and assist them in finding their footing in all the other aspects covered by the houses at the bottom of the chart. Children learn by example and experience, and it is generally a mother's job to teach these aspects of life.

If Saturn is at the top of the chart, higher than the sun and the moon, the child viewed their mother as the dominant parent. This can appear if the father worked away, as the mother would have control of the family unit for long periods of time, or if the family was without an obvious father figure.

Saturn on the "me" side of the chart indicates either a mother who was afraid of failing as a parent (particularly if Saturn is in the twelfth or first house) or a mother who was too self-contained or detached to be approachable. If Saturn is in the ninth house, the mother was seen as clever. This is not necessarily negative, but it would give the child a feeling of either having to compete intellectually or a disinclination to attempt to compete. Either way, this position engenders an atmosphere of competition not conducive to a close and loving bond. If Saturn is in tenth house, the mother may have worked a lot and left the child with others to be looked after, or the mother was too tired or busy when she was home to be able to give the child the tender affection they required.

Saturn right on the AC (ascendant) or very close to it (within a few degrees) means the mother figure attempted to protect the child from situations that might cause harm. This is not always a bad thing, but the child was not given the opportunity to learn for themselves. Having a very overprotective mother likely gave the child a feeling of threat from many sources, so they might grow up to be fearful of new situations and people.

Saturn right on the DC (descendant) or very close to it is also perceived as overprotective, but here the mother is attempting to protect the child from others. She may use the child as her own companion, choose whom the child can be friends with, or inhibit contact with those that she thinks unsuitable, leaving the child with an inability to make their own judgments about others.

## The Moon (The Child)

The ideal position of the moon is on the DC (descendant), or in houses six through eight, where it can meet others.

If the moon is high in a birth chart, the child needed praise and appreciation. If it is the highest of the three planets, the child's parents had high expectations for them; the child was constantly praised, even when unwarranted or unnecessary. This put pressure on the child to show their talents and abilities to the world and thus fulfil their parents' high expectations. Remember, this is the "being in the public eye" section of the chart, so the parents expected their child to shine in the world.

If the moon is on the IC or in the fourth house, the child will feel secure and at home with their family, and they will carry this need for their parents throughout their life. This may not necessarily appear dependent or needy; the child will be supportive and helpful to the parents, especially in old age. Some children may cling to their parents, but this will depend on the child's individual chart.

The Hubers thought a low moon could indicate suppression by the parents. Or, in the fourth house, a surfeit of love that made it difficult for the child to leave home. Certainly, if the moon is in fourth house, the home and family is of incredible importance throughout the child's life, and there will be a constant seesawing of emotions while trying to separate themselves from their roots in order to create a separate household.

Moon on the AC or in the twelfth/first house shows a child who preferred to go to their room to be alone, a private and introverted child. Bear in mind that someone with the moon hidden away on the AC or in the twelfth house will be emotionally detached from people, so it certainly could create difficulties later in life.

## Other Notes

Of the sun, moon, and Saturn, which planet is highest? This shows whom the child saw as being the most important member of the family.

Are all three planets in the same quadrant? This indicates a close family, though not necessarily a harmonious one.

If the moon is separated across the chart from either the sun or Saturn, this suggests a child at variance with that parent or that the child felt distant from them.

Aspects between these three planets are also important. The Hubers found that a direct aspect usually indicated tension, to a certain extent.

A square or opposition (red aspect lines) between the sun and Saturn indicates parents who were always arguing or competing. The square would have been visible to the child, while the opposition was tension beneath the surface.

The conjunction of the moon and either the sun or Saturn can be good or bad. It is a strong tie but may leave the child with an inability to identify their own feelings. Because they were wrapped up in their parent's emotions and life, the child will find themselves unable to separate the two when older and independent. A moon/Saturn conjunction can leave the child with lifelong feelings of guilt.

Blue aspects between the moon and either parent (sun/Saturn) are easier, but they indicate that the child felt obliged to do as they were told. The sextile, especially, made the child feel there was something expected of them.

Green aspects between the moon and the sun or Saturn plant doubt in the child's mind as to where they stand in relation to the parent. It might indicate a longing for a relationship that wasn't there, or an idealised view of the child/parent bond.

If there are no aspects between the sun, moon, or Saturn at all, the child was not aware that any inner relationship existed. It could be that one parent was literally missing: away at work, dead, or had left the family home.

$$☽ \ast ☾$$

Check out your own chart and see what you think. Does the Family Model help you make sense of your relationship with your father and mother figure during childhood?

Did they expect a lot of you (high moon) or were they too involved with each other (conjunction of sun/Saturn) to spend much time with you? Were you allowed to meet and play with others (moon on or near DC) or protected/overprotected (Saturn on or near AC/DC)? Where did you see yourself in relation to your parents? Which of the three planets is highest?

What sort of relationship did you have with your father figure? Did you admire him (sun high in the chart) or feel he failed you (sun low)? Can you see how the element of the sun sign reflected how you perceived him?

And what about your mother or mother figure? Did she overly protect you (Saturn close to AC or DC), compete with you (Saturn in ninth house), or was she too busy working to spend much time with you (Saturn in tenth)? Or was Saturn in the perfect place—houses two through five—so that your mother figure provided the nurturing and support you needed?

Because we role model based on our childhood family dynamics when we create our own family, the Family Model is quite an important psychological tool in understanding things we rarely consciously consider. Unless we had a particularly difficult childhood, or a really happy one, often we don't think about it, yet it will form our own beliefs as to how a mother and father should behave in a family unit. Have you gone on to recreate the same type of family dynamics? Self-knowledge can help us to avoid things that caused us stress/distress as a child and consciously choose to live a different way in our own family unit.

Part III
**USING YOUR SKILLS**

## Eleven

# RELATIONSHIPS AND
# CAREER INFORMATION

*T*hese are the two parts of a birth chart that people are most interested in, so let's have a look at them in-depth.

## Relationships in a Chart

Relationship issues form the most common questions an astrologer receives. For example: "What sort of person would suit me?" "Is my current or prospective partner worth taking a chance on?" and "Why do I keep making the same mistakes when choosing a partner?"

In fact, our birth chart provides great insight on the sort of partner we seek and who will suit us best. The relationship houses are the fifth and the seventh. The fifth house covers love affairs, and the seventh deals with long-term partnerships.

Whenever you look at anyone's chart to see what they seek in relationships, check the following points. Later, we will cover synastry, which is simply comparing two charts to see if the individuals are compatible. But for now, start with your own chart to find the type of partner who suits you best.

Pull up your chart and go through the following points. Make notes to help you remember.

## 1. What Astrological Sign Is in the Seventh House?

This shows the type of partner you seek. Is the seventh house in a fire, earth, air, or water sign? Most people end up with a partner whose sun sign is literally the same as their seventh house sign, but finding a partner whose sign is the same element is also highly likely.

However, sometimes we end up with partners who don't have any link to our seventh house sign. When this happens it is usually because there are other aspects that are compelling to you in their chart. For example, those who marry for security rather than love often choose a partner who reflects their fourth house sign and/or element, but even if that is missing, there may be Venus or Mars links. These aspects will be discussed later, and they will also be talked about in chapter 13.

So, when checking your own chart, your ideal long-term partner is one who reflects your seventh house sign in some way. If it's Aries, you seek a fire-sign type. You may also find a Leo or Sagittarius appealing because they express the fire qualities of action and independence. If your partner isn't a fire sun sign, they may have personal planets in a fire sign. It may not be clear-cut at first glance, but there is no doubt you will be drawn to a fire-sign type of person, someone who expresses that type of energy in some way.

Another very strong link is someone who has the sun or moon in your first house, in your ascending sign. This is often regarded as karmic, so there will be past-life issues to resolve. Despite being very drawn to this person, they may not be your final, long-term partner.

## 2. What Planets, if Any, Are in the Seventh House?

Planets in a house draw us to that area, so any planet in the seventh house indicates a strong interest in forming partnerships.

If there is a planet in the seventh house, which is it? Remember, the seventh house planets will be on an angle and in an important house; that planet will know how to get what it wants.

To recap, the sun gets its sense of identity from the partner, so the sun in the seventh house is consciously looking for someone. The moon in the seventh house wants and needs an emotional connection. Mercury is seeking someone they can relate to intellectually and talk about shared interests with. Venus will have a strong desire for a calm, balanced, and fair partnership; Venus rules Libra, whose symbol is the scales, and Libra is the ruler of the seventh house, so Venus is a lovely planet to have here. Mars will be driven to find a life partner, and Jupiter will only feel truly alive when in a partnership. Uranus will be unpredictable and will change partners often or choose unusual partners. Neptune will be unrealistic in their expectations and may be misled by partners. Pluto will want to control partners.

Saturn, which is always a special case, will choose an older partner or someone traditional and settled (Capricorn-like). Because Saturn is a fear area, these people have a lot of difficulties with relationships, so refer back to chapter 7 to find out how it affects people when placed in the seventh house.

If there aren't planets in the seventh house, that doesn't mean the individual will be unable to find a partner. The individual will still look for a partner with the same astrological sign as their seventh house, or certainly the same element, but this area of life will not be a priority for them.

### 3. Check the Fifth House

What sign and planets (if any) are in the fifth house? This house covers a lot of different aspects, so unlike the seventh house, it will not be possible to pinpoint a direct link to relationships. But certainly, if there is a planet here, it will draw you to this house—especially if there is no planet in the seventh.

Because the fifth house rules creativity, personal planets in this house can obviously express themselves through art, acting, or a musical endeavour, but very often these areas offer romantic opportunities, so any planet here will always have an eye on this aspect. Planets here show there is a preference for a lively life and mixing with lots of people, and inevitably, relationships will be formed. However, relationships formed are unlikely to be lasting for exactly the same reason: other opportunities for liaisons abound.

This house also shows a person's attitude toward having children. This is not as cut-and-dried as, say, having a fire sign in the seventh house, because there are many things that can influence a person's desire to have a family. But certainly, if Saturn is in the fifth house, there may be an inability or reluctance to have children and a general fear of expressing their fun side.

If there is no planet in the fifth house, this does not mean people won't have children, but there may be less of a compelling desire. They may have children because it is expected in society or because family members put pressure on them. For someone who has a brood of children, it is rare to see no planets in the fifth house. However, there will often be other pointers in a chart; even without planets in the fifth house, a person whose fifth house is in Cancer, Capricorn, or Taurus may want children, as some signs are more family-minded than others.

If someone has no planets in the seventh house and a few in the fifth, they may prefer to have brief liaisons, but that doesn't mean they won't ever settle down. What it *does* mean is that they may be older before they settle down, and because their natural inclination is to be more lighthearted in relationships, they may have difficulty staying in a relationship for a lifetime.

Interpreting charts is not always straightforward. Sometimes it involves taking everything in the chart into account and using your judgment to assess the possibilities. For example, if someone has Uranus in the seventh house, they will be drawn to a long-term relationship. They might actually choose an Aquarian (because Uranus rules Aquarius) or someone who is different in some way, or just another air sign. Even so, Uranus is disruptive and needs change, so in the seventh house it suggests the person will commit to a partnership but may abruptly end it. This could happen after forty years or just two.

### 4. Assess Feelings about Money and Finances

Money and finances are incredibly important. One of the most common arguments between couples is about their finances, so this is where chart information really comes into play! Check the second house. If there is no planet here, look at the second house's astrological sign for clues about someone's relationship with money. If there is a planet here, it will speak volumes about how they feel about money.

So, which sign is in your second house? Are you driven to create security? (This is best represented by an earth sign or any personal planet in the second house, but especially the sun or moon.) If so, it's best to avoid partners who are spendthrifts or lackadaisical about money; think Aquarius, Sagittarius, Leo, Libra, or Aries in the second house. If you are casual or vague about money (all of the above plus Pisces or Gemini), you will struggle to get along with partners who are hoarders (Capricorn, Taurus, Virgo, or Cancer in the second house). Remember Saturn, too—watch out for a partner with Saturn here. They will strive to make money but will rarely achieve their goal. The same goes for anyone whose Saturn sits in the second house.

## 5. Where Are the North and South Nodes?

Look at your birth chart. Do the placements of your north and south nodes deal with relationships? If so, does the house of the north node mean you are supposed to be avoiding commitment, or are you meant to be learning how to form relationships? This is shown by the north nodes in the first and seventh houses. Look back at the information on the nodes in chapter 9 to refresh your memory if you need to.

Should you be looking for someone who can look after you, or are you learning to stand on your own two feet financially? This is shown by the north nodes in the second or eighth house. Where is your comfort zone (south node), and what challenges will life present you with (north node)? Knowing the answers to these questions helps greatly when making future choices about relationships.

## 6. Check the General Feel of the Chart

The chart's aspect lines show if you are active or relaxed. Are you active (red), laid-back or outright lazy (all blue and green or too much blue), or inclined to be snappy and irritable (mostly red and green)? The latter may create someone who relaxes by doing something active, so partners need to have a lot of energy to keep up!

When checking the chart of a prospective partner, it might be useful to know whether they complement your own attitude to activity and relaxation. I've known relationships that have failed because one partner wanted to stay in bed until mid-morning and the other was raring to go out and enjoy the day three hours earlier. Sharing activities and days out are an important part of a fulfilling relationship. Always doing things alone provides opportunities to meet others who are more of a like mind.

## 7. Look at the Planet Balance

Which area (quadrant) are you happiest in? In other words, where are most of your personal planets? If you are someone who has a lot of planets in the fifth house and wants an active social life, it is pointless to choose a "me"-sided person (someone with planets on the far left) who likes peace and quiet. However, if you are more of a bottom-of-the-chart person and your partner is more a top-of-the-chart person, this can function perfectly well as long as you are aware that your partner likes to spend time alone, and as long as "rules" about finding time to enjoy things together as a couple are drawn up at the start. A top-of-the-chart person can adapt, but a left, me-sided person cannot, because being alone is such an intrinsic part of their personality.

## 8. Check Out the Moon and Venus

Locate the moon and Venus. What are your emotional needs (the sign and house of the moon)? It is very important for the moons of two people to be harmoniously linked, but this is dealt with in chapter 13, the synastry chapter. For now, check out what you want based on your moon and Venus signs and houses. Venus is how you love, so the astrological sign will tell a lot about how you love in a personal sense, and the house Venus is in is where you express your loving, caring side in the outside world.

Self-knowledge helps us make more considered choices in relationships. If we know we are active, casual about money, and prefer to work alone with a "me"-sided chart, there is no point in starting a relationship with someone who is a couch potato, obsessed with saving money, wants to go into business with their romantic partner, and enjoys a lively social life. It's like that old saying, "Know thyself," in action. Once we understand what we want and need from a partner, we make better, more informed choices, and we are less likely to suffer future heartbreak.

☽ ✳ ☾

Apply your new knowledge about relationships by looking at your own birth chart first. Then have a go at someone else's—a friend, family member, or partner—but make sure you are looking at the birth chart of someone who is perfectly sure of their birth time.

# Career Information in a Chart

The houses concerned with work and career are the sixth and the tenth. The difference between them is that the sixth house is behind-the-scenes, unsung work, whereas the tenth house denotes a professional career that is in the public eye. By looking at your birth chart, you can determine if you are in the right job. If you are dissatisfied, your chart might well show a career path that would suit you better or provide more fulfilment. These are the things to consider:

## 1. Look at the Sixth and Tenth Houses

What astrological signs are in the sixth and tenth houses? Based on these signs, how do you feel about each area? For example, if these are fire signs you might want an active career that offers challenges. Air signs mean you will be more interested in information technology and anything that entails words, communication, and language. You will probably be good at technical things too. Water signs mean you will seek a career that makes a difference, one that has a caring aspect to it—certainly one that offers fulfilment beyond earning a living. Earth signs here indicate you seek a stable, secure profession where you can stay for a long time; you will dislike change.

Are there any planets in the sixth house? Even one personal planet in the sixth house will show a willingness to be of service, and the sun here indicates someone who gets their sense of identity from doing things for other people. It is Virgo's house, so any planet here will have a service/dutiful feel. There is a lot of information on the sixth house—and planets placed there—in chapter 3, so check back if you have forgotten.

Is there a planet on the MC or in the tenth house? A planet right on the MC (or within two degrees) shows a strong need to express itself through that house, but any planet in the tenth house will draw you to a career rather than just a job. If there is a planet on the MC or in the tenth house, is it a ruler? This will give you more confidence and competence and a natural ability to be in charge. If there are planets in both the sixth and tenth houses, you may choose a career that has a service feel, but you will want more than a behind-the-scenes role. Nevertheless, you will be willing to undertake any role—however menial—if necessary.

## 2. Where Is Mars?

Mars is significant when it comes to career. Mars is our life force and drive, remember? What sign and house is Mars in?

In the past, women were actively discouraged from expressing their Mars energy. It was seen as "too masculine." Because of cultural rules they were often blocked from a clear career path, and many professions were not open to them. Each country in the world had (and has) different expectations of women's roles, but women have only recently been encouraged to forge a career, even in the Western world. But it was not just women who struggled to express their true selves. Before the internet, information was difficult to find and young people were often pushed into traditional, "safe" jobs. Also, people found it difficult to choose unusual careers; careers like acting and art were considered unsuitable. The farther we look back in time, the less people in general were able to express their Mars energy in the way they would have liked to. So do bear this in mind when looking at the chart of an older person or someone who, for whatever reason, may have been (or be) unable to follow their dreams. Look at their chart to determine the career that would have suited them, then find out what they did do. See how they adapted to fit in with society's expectations and what aspects of their chart they activated to find a life they were comfortable with.

## 3. What Planets, if Any, Are in the Second House?

The second house is particularly significant because it shows a person's attitude toward money and possessions. Is there a planet in the second house? Are you driven to make money? Remember, those with the sun in the second house are often millionaires (or at least comfortably well-off) because they get their sense of identity from money and possessions. With that being said, any planet in the second house will show an interest in money, possessions, and security, so it is rare to find someone with a planet here who is work-shy or a dropout.

## 4. Look at the Quadrant Emphasis

Are you happy being in the collective (working in the community/the area below the AC/DC line)? Or are you drawn to higher institutions like universities and careers that involve investigation and research (planets in the ninth house)? Do you want a career that makes a difference in people's lives (planets in the eleventh house)? Do you prefer to work from home (sun in the fourth house) or to serve others (sun in the sixth house)?

While it is not always possible to predict an exact career by looking at a birth chart, these motivations will provide a good starting point for choosing a suitable occupation.

## 5. Analyse Other Planetary Positions

If the sun or another strong planet (Mars, Jupiter, or even spiritual Neptune) is in twelfth house, this suggests that solitary careers are of interest. These could be careers related to religions, hospitals, or prisons, or perhaps working on a remote island for a charity.

Is there a strong fifth-house planet? Medical professions and carers fall under this house, but they often have a planet in the sixth house, too, because they serve humanity by helping patients get better. Artistic endeavours are shown in the fifth house, so writers, artists, musicians, and people who enjoy being creative will have a planet here. Creativity covers many areas: fashion design, furniture making, party organising, being a children's entertainer— anything that allows someone to express themselves and their ideas falls under the fifth house. Lots of "look at me" planets in the fifth house might indicate the desire to be an actor (Leo emphasis). Leo sun in the tenth house will describe a showy, larger-than-life person who enjoys being centre stage in their career.

The sun in the first house or right on the AC line is someone no one can ignore. They often shine in life and become well-known, so they will certainly have a high-profile career.

## 6. Find the North and South Nodes

Does the north node position indicate that you are meant to forge a career, or are you supposed to be focused on the fourth house of home and family? (Look for fourth/tenth house nodes.)

Are you a teacher? Sun or Mars in third house, especially in the sign of Gemini, are the aspects to look for. Third/ninth house nodes indicate a student (who may also have the sun or Mars in ninth house) or a teacher (third-house north node).

Are you meant to be rolling up your sleeves and working behind the scenes (sun or Mars in sixth house and/or the sixth/twelfth house nodes), or are you meant to retreat to find your spiritual meaning (sun or Mars in twelfth house and/or those with the sixth/twelfth house nodes)?

Bear in mind the south node and where the individual feels comfortable because this is probably where they would prefer to be (and maybe still are). Some people may be dipping their toe into their north node and some may already be there. Take all of this into account when analysing a career choice for someone else.

# Twelve
# *A FULL CHART INTERPRETATION*

**N**ow that you have spent so much time looking at your own chart, this is the time to give a new one a try. If you haven't already looked at another person's chart, ask someone you know well if you can use theirs. Remember, for a birth chart reading to be accurate, the individual must know their exact time of birth.

Print out the birth chart, then work through it step-by-step, making notes as you go. Have a go at the planets, signs, and houses—even the aspects, if you feel able. And don't panic!

## Interpreting a Birth Chart

Looking at a new chart for the first time is scary. Your initial reaction might be that you can't possibly interpret it. Actually, you can. The secret is to take your time. Follow these points, make notes, and by the end, you will have done it.

A word of advice: you will be dealing with people's innermost motivations, desires, fear areas, and karmic lessons. An empathic, understanding, and non-judgmental approach is essential. Never show surprise, no matter what you see or hear. Never offer any opinions of your own, or make suggestions, unless you are asked. And even then, base the answers on what is in their chart, not on your own beliefs or thoughts. Your job is to help another understand themselves, not to judge them, and certainly not to solve their problems for them.

### 1. Start with the Basics

How many of their planets are in fire, earth, air, and water? Which do they have the most of? This will describe the individual's basic drive. Are they action takers (fire), security-minded (earth), caring (water), or information seekers/teachers (air)?

Now check to see how many of those planets are in cardinal, fixed, or mutable signs to see if they are proactive, prefer the status quo, or are flexible. Already you will start to see the type of person they are. Then work out the elements and motivations in the houses to see what the world is expecting them to be.

### 2. Look at the Quadrants

Which area is the individual operating in? Are they a "me" person or an "others" person? Are they in the collective community section, or up in the individual thinking/actions for others area? This is a very important tool in assessing someone's innate drives and needs.

If you see a chart with all left-sided planets—and especially if they have a red opposition line running from top to bottom, effectively cutting them off from the right-hand side of the chart—you can be sure they are loners who have little need for others. In contrast, all right-sided planets (and maybe a red opposition line blocking them from the left side of the chart) means they desperately need other people and dislike being alone.

These are the two extremes. Most of us have a scattering of planets and can work in a few areas. But always keep an eye out for a chart that is very focused in one particular area, because they have difficulty with areas they have no planets in.

### 3. What Is the Ascendant?

How are they presenting themselves? The ascendant or rising sign, as it is otherwise known, is a very important tool for understanding people. But it is not just about the astrological sign. How someone presents themselves also depends on if there are any planets in the first house because these planets will be presented immediately. Remember, Venus here will be charming, Mars a bit aggressive, Jupiter will make them a bit over-the-top, the moon will be very receptive to others, and so forth. And the sun in the first house is a very strong position; it is impossible not to notice someone with the sun here.

## 4. Analyse the Planet Positions by Sign and House

Start with the sun. What is the individual's sun sign and in what area (house) are they expressing their unique identity?

How do they relate emotionally? (Moon by sign and house.)

How do they think? (Mercury by sign and house.)

How do they love? (Venus by sign and house.)

What is their ambition? Where are they driven to succeed? (Mars by sign and house.)

Where do they get the most joy? (Jupiter by sign and house.)

Are there planets on angles? Are they sure of themselves or not?

Where are the outer planets? In what area is Neptune causing confusion? Where is Uranus upsetting the apple cart? And where is Pluto demanding control?

Are any of their planets in a house without a cusp (intercepted)? How do you think this might affect them?

## 5. Look at the Aspect Lines

Based on the individual's aspect patterns, are they active, lazy, or dreamy, or do they have a good balance of aspect colours? Do they have any difficult aspects, like oppositions? If so, which planets are involved?

Look at any important aspect patterns—the ones described in chapter 6. Someone with an efficiency triangle will be a hard worker, but which planet is at the apex of this energetic triangle, and in which house are they working hard? The grand trine shows a natural talent. What talent might that be, do you think? And if the aspect patterns are red and green, you can be sure that no matter how pleasant a person may seem, they are easily irritated!

## 6. Assess the Fear Area

What is their fear area (Saturn) by sign and house? What does this tell you? Saturn is such an important planet to assess in a chart, so be sure to take time figuring out what it is saying. It is easy to dismiss someone's fears and worries if they are things that wouldn't bother us, but they are very real to the person who has them.

Someone who has Saturn in the second house might spend their lives working, yet achieve very little in the way of financial reward. This can be heartbreaking and soul-destroying for them, just as those who have Saturn in the seventh house may despair of their relationships—how is it that everyone else seems to get it right, but they can't? Always be compassionate and understanding when handling someone else's chart interpretation.

## 7. Utilise the Family Model

What does the Family Model tell you about the individual's childhood?

Which planet is highest: the sun, moon, or Saturn? How might this have affected their adult life? Have they recreated the same family model they grew up with, and is it causing difficulties? Self-knowledge and awareness will help them make better decisions and choices in the future.

## 8. Where Are They by Age Point?

This seems irrelevant sometimes when interpreting a chart, but it really is important to find out where they are in their chart, and in their lives. Remember, the house they are going through will be the focus of their thoughts and actions, and the sign will describe how they feel; energetic if fire, intellectual or in study mode if air, needing to put down roots or create security if earth, and, if it's a water sign, all their emotions will be heightened. Any planets their age point crosses will be activated.

Once, I had a mother come to me regarding her toddler son. He was aggressive and difficult, and his age point was on Mars in the first house. The poor little lad was trying to grapple with Mars energy before he could handle it. Knowing this, the mother tried to direct his energy into positive action so that he could work off this excess energy and drive in a constructive way. She was relieved to hear it wasn't going to last a lifetime, but was just a passing phase!

### 9. What Are the Positions of the North and South Nodes?

Obviously, this is the most important aspect of a chart in defining where their life direction should be, and where they have come from.

Most people readily accept the idea of a previous life, but always stress that this is a theory and they must judge for themselves. Being given a chart is a gesture of trust. Use your knowledge and wisdom kindly and with empathy, and never force your own beliefs on someone else, no matter how many times your beliefs have proven themselves to you or how confident you feel in them.

### 10. Look at the Relationship Houses

Have a look at their relationship houses (fifth and seventh) and decide what sort of partner they will look for and be happy with. Even if they are in a long-term, apparently settled partnership, they may have chosen to go against their innate feelings because of the fear of being alone, because of financial security, or any number of other reasons, so try to be objective and ignore what you think you already know about them. Analyse the chart and impart only the information it gives you. And don't be afraid to say they like short liaisons if they have a busy fifth house! There are nice ways to say difficult things, and chart interpretation involves a steep learning curve in expressing things in a nonjudgmental, empathic way.

For example, a young woman once came to me who had no planets in the seventh house but four planets in the fifth, one of which was the sun. The sign was Taurus. This suggested she earned security and money from fifth-house activities and that she enjoyed brief relationships. It turned out that she sold her "favours" for money and had four children by different men. Her sun here showed she got her sense of identity from this, and she was not at all abashed to admit this was what she did and that she liked living this way. Her north nodes were in the fifth house, too, so she was following the right path for her, and she was learning much about relating to others in this life. So, to reiterate, never judge or condemn, because we are all on different paths and have different lessons to learn. There is no right or wrong in a birth chart—there are just differences.

## 11. Look at the Career Houses

Check their career houses (sixth and tenth) and decide whether they want a career or not. Do they want to serve others or be in control? Are they happier behind the scenes (sixth house planets) or are they seeking a high-profile career (tenth house planets)? How do they feel about money (second house), and where is Mars? Based on the astrological signs in the sixth and tenth houses, what sort of job might they like? Active, intellectual, traditional, or caring? What sort of job might they be happy doing?

$$\text{☽} * \text{☾}$$

That's it! You've done it. You've fully interpreted a birth chart. Well done!

At first, charts take a long time to interpret. This first one may have taken you hours. But don't be disheartened, because it really does get easier and quicker the more you do.

My experience reading birth charts goes back years, so now my eye instantly takes in the quadrant information, the aspect colours and patterns, the ascendant and the sun and moon, and even the nodes. Within a few minutes, I already have a good idea of what the chart is saying. Even so, chart reading still requires studying in-depth because it's important not to miss a vital bit of information. So, never hurry a chart, but be aware that it won't take you hours forever!

## Example of a Full Chart Interpretation: Abraham Lincoln

Abraham Lincoln's birth chart is truly fascinating and provides good practise on areas we have looked at in this book. Let's work through the points as described above.

## 1. Start with the Basics

Having counted Abraham's planets, he had four in the element of water and five in mutable signs, making him very Piscean by birth. That means he was nonjudgmental, accepting of everyone, and had a farseeing, spiritual belief in all of humanity; he would have valued every single person as much as the next. His innate personality would have been kindly, compassionate, and understanding.

Name: ♂ Abraham Lincoln
born on Su., 12 February 1809
in Hodgenville, KY (US)
85w44, 37n34

Natal Chart (Method: Huber / Koch)

Time:        6:54 a.m. LMT
Univ.Time: 12:36:56
Sid. Time:  16:22:34

ASTRO⊙DIENST
www.astro.com

Type: 2.H  0.0-1  10-Sep-2021

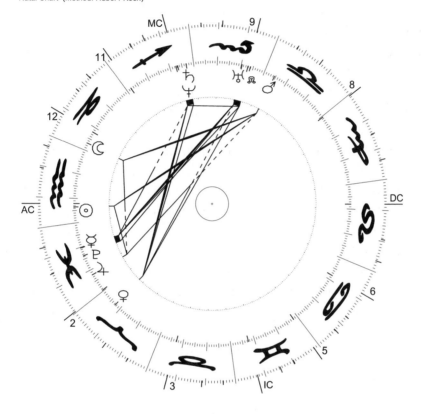

| ☉ 23≈27' | ♀ 7♈28' | ♄ 3♐ 9' | ♇ 13⊀37' | AC 22≈ 5' |
| ☽ 27♉ 0' | ♂ 25♎30' | ♅ 9≏40' | ☊ 6♏10' | MC 7♐27' |
| ☿ 10⊀18' | ♃ 22⊀ 5' | ♆ 6♐41' | ⚷ 11≈44' | |

But when we look at the count of planets in the houses, we see the world wanted cardinal fire from him. That is Aries, ruled by the planet of war, Mars—the world required him to fight.

## 2. Look at the Quadrants

Abraham's chart is clearly "me" sided. This made him self-contained and self-reliant, unable to fully relate to people in a personal way. However, his planets in the eighth, ninth, and tenth houses show he could comfortably engage with others in a professional setting.

He had a lot of planets in the impulsive section. These planets were in Aquarius/Pisces, which are detached but humanitarian signs—his innate impulses in this instance would have been for the good of the whole.

The other cluster of planets are up in the individual thinking section, and with Mars in Libra, too, Abraham analysed and considered all his actions and made every effort to be reasoned, fair, and balanced in his dealings with people. Plus, he had an overview of life from this higher perspective.

## 3. What Is the Ascendant?

Abraham's ascendant was Aquarius. This made him unafraid of rocking the boat, shocking people, or going against what was seen as normal behaviour at the time. Like Pisces, Aquarius is impartial, open-minded, and accepting of all, but Aquarius adds a humanitarian bent to the mix; also, Aquarius has a desire to shake people out of their complacency. Both signs are emotionally detached and cool.

## 4. Analyse their Planet Positions by Sign and House

Let's look at his planets by sign and house. Saturn will be discussed later, in the section about fear areas.

### SUN

The sun is on his ascendant, so this was the first thing people saw. Because his sun was in the first house, Abraham could not hide behind his ascending sign. He was who he was, and he was unafraid of showing his true self. He fully expressed his sun and the characteristics of the sign of Aquarius.

The sun is on an angle, the AC. In chapter 8, we learned that this means he was confident, unruffled, and sure of himself. He obviously presented himself as completely sure of his own talents and abilities, and this inner confidence would have been alluring to others, who no doubt perceived him as a willing and able leader of men. Remember, planets on the AC have a clear idea of their own personal abilities and feel no need to prove themselves or be something they are not. This is an extremely strong position for the sun, as it cannot be ignored.

### MOON

His moon is in Capricorn in the twelfth house. Twelfth house planets are kept solely for the use of the individual, so Abraham was unable to link emotionally to another person in a personal way. This is intensified by his chart being so "me" sided and the bulk of his personal planets being in signs that were spiritual and humanitarian. His whole outlook was impersonal. That does not mean he was unloving, but that the love in his heart was directed toward the entire human race rather than at an individual level.

The moon in Capricorn gave him a traditional view of religion (it's in the twelfth house of spiritual matters), a belief in the basic structures of civilisation, and the need for stability and continuance. This view of religion was expanded by his Aquarius/Pisces emphasis, but he still needed the basic, traditionally accepted structure of beliefs as building blocks.

### MERCURY

His Mercury was in Pisces in the first house. He was unafraid of speaking his mind and comfortable expressing his thoughts to others because of this first house position. But in Pisces, others would have been aware of the sweetness and kindness that typifies this sign. He had a love of his fellow man and an accepting-of-all manner.

Note that Pluto is conjunct Mercury, empowering it with a Scorpio-like depth and passion. He was no doubt an impassioned speaker, able to rouse people to his cause. Because both his Mercury and Pluto were water signs, this lent an emotional, caring quality to his words; listeners would have found it hard not to be moved. Mercury is linked by trine aspect to Neptune, which is on the MC (midheaven). Neptune is the ruler of Pisces, so he would have had the ability to utilise these powerful, compassionate words to aid his career.

### VENUS

Venus was in Aries, the second house of finances and possessions. In times gone by, men had to express their more feminine side through the females in their lives, so we look at Venus to see the type of woman he would have found interesting. In Aries, he sought a fire sign, a feisty woman who also had money (because Venus was in the second house). I will expand on this more in the following section on relationships.

### MARS

Mars is in Libra in the eighth house. Before he was a politician, Abraham was a lawyer. Libra corresponds with the legal profession because of its need to balance opposing views and find compromises. It is also in the eighth house, which is the house of other people's money, possessions, values, and ideals. The eighth house traditionally deals with death and inheritances, too. So, it makes a lot of sense that he became a lawyer.

Mars is especially important in a man's chart to describe their life force and drive. This position shows how reasoned and balanced Abraham was. He would have been a fair person to deal with. He was so good at his job that he became a renowned lawyer and commanded high fees to represent people.

It is interesting that Mars had a square aspect to the moon. A square is working energy, but both Libra and Capricorn are calm and logical. Both seek the higher financial ground, so the moon would have spurred Mars to achieve professional (and thus, financial) success.

### JUPITER

Jupiter was in Pisces, which would have given Abraham a feeling of compassionate love for all with an innate belief in the connectedness of all people from all walks of life. He would have been sensitive to other people's feelings and would have intuitively known how to handle them.

Because Jupiter was in the first house, it also imbued him with enthusiasm and courage when leading others. He was someone who created opportunities and who grabbed them when they were presented. He would have been his own best advertisement.

### URANUS

Uranus is the ruler of Abraham's ascendant and sun, and its position in the ninth house shows an unusual approach to higher learning. It linked with a trine aspect to Mercury in the first house; it is interesting that Abraham was a self-taught man. He grew up on a farm and had no consistent teaching. Most boys in that position would have taken over the farm, but he chose to study the law. For all of his life he was an avid reader and writer of poetry, most unusual in a poorly educated farm boy; this was unpredictable Uranus doing things differently.

Despite his humble origins, he pursued his ambitions (Mars in Libra in the eighth house) and was not afraid to be different. Uranus was in Scorpio, so this learning and research was obviously something he felt passionate about. Studying in-depth would have been a delight to him.

### NEPTUNE

The position of Neptune in the tenth house gave Abraham dreams of having a meaningful career, one that changed the lives of people for the better. He would have relied heavily on his intuition and gut instinct in his pursuit of making the world a better, fairer place. Neptune in Sagittarius gave Abraham the ability to flexibly change his ideas and opinions. Perhaps he sometimes spread himself too thin trying to be all things to all people, but his heart would have been in the right place. This placement also indicates he was unafraid of speaking the truth, no matter how unpalatable.

### PLUTO

Pluto was conjunct Mercury in the first house. This would have imbued his speech with a mesmerising power and an intensity of drive and purpose. This also gave him a deep intuition. His drive to express himself would have been immense, yet subtle because Pluto is not showy. Abraham would have been an incredibly impassioned speaker, able to sway an audience—a very useful ability for both a lawyer and a politician.

## 5. Look at the Aspect Lines

Can you see how dreamy and idealistic he was? He had seven blue aspects and five green. All those blue and green aspect lines reflect his Aquarius/ Pisces idealism.

Abraham had two red aspects: squares between Mars and the moon and between Mercury and Saturn. This gave him some much-needed working energy. The square between Mercury and Saturn advised caution, attempting to teach him to be careful of expressing too many of his unusual or outrageous thoughts. Issuing the Emancipation Proclamation went against many people's beliefs at the time; Abraham chose his battles, and this was the one he decided to pursue. Had he lived a longer life, who knows what further bastions he would have toppled in due course.

## 6. Assess the Fear Area

Saturn was right on the midheaven, the MC. Remember, MC planets want to control and take charge of a group. They inwardly feel perfectly capable of being in charge, and this confidence inspires others to believe in them. MC planets have a sense of destiny. *They know where they are going.*

This strong position of Saturn in the sign of Sagittarius shows he had basic traditional beliefs (reinforced by Capricorn in the twelfth house) and was unwilling to involve himself in other religions or beliefs. His humanitarian aims may have been out of sync with the times, but they had their basis in the traditional biblical teachings of the day.

Saturn here traditionally means many setbacks on the way to power. It also imbues the individual with a desire to rule alone and a fear of failure. Neptune conjunct Saturn reinforced this uncertainty deep in his soul: uncertainty about whether he was doing the right thing; uncertainty about whether he was following the right path; uncertainty that he had the power to lead and change the world. Everyone struggles with some form of self-questioning, and this aspect shows that deep down, Abraham confronted as many fears and insecurities as everyone about life and our chosen path.

## 7. Utilise the Family Model

We can see that the sun (Abraham's father) was on the AC, that the moon (Abraham) was tucked away in the twelfth house, and that Saturn (his mother) was the highest planet, right up on the MC.

Abraham had a difficult relationship with his father due to his father's unreliability and lackadaisical attitude to work. He often made Abraham do all the work on the farm and even hired him out to others and took Abraham's pay away from him. The sun was the lowest of the three family planets, suggesting Abraham felt his father failed him. It is close to the AC, which shows his father was an introspective, reserved person whom Abraham struggled to get to know and respect. His father's unpredictability and emotional detachment are epitomised by the sun being in Aquarius.

Saturn (his mother), on the other hand, was the highest and most respected of the family planets. There is no doubt the ideal position of Saturn is at the bottom of the chart, so at the top, it suggests his mother worked hard and had little quality time available. Nevertheless, it shows he viewed his mother as the intellectually superior person of the family unit.

Abraham himself was a loner. The moon in the twelfth house indicates a child who prefers to be alone and often seeks out solitude.

All three planets are in the same quadrant, but there are no links (aspect lines) between any of them, suggesting that they got along as best they could without any outright arguments. Because Abraham's mother died when he was so young, the lack of an aspect line and his moon in the twelfth house reveal his loneliness and isolation. It is fitting that he eventually broke contact with his father and did not attend his funeral.

## 8. Where Are They by Age Point?

When Abraham died, he was fifty-six. By age point, he had just passed his MC Saturn/Neptune conjunction. Saturn in the tenth house does mean a fall from power at some stage, but it does not indicate death as a means.

By age point, Abraham was passing through the sign of Sagittarius, so it's likely he had many projects he wanted to push forward with and anticipated an active and rewarding period in his life.

## 9. What Are the Positions of the North and South Nodes?

Abraham's north node was in Scorpio in the ninth house. Most people have no desire to reach their north node house, but with two planets (Mars and Uranus) here, he was drawn toward it. The ninth house is all about higher learning and finding one's own philosophies and truth. It is telling that he took to private study, which is very much ninth-house behaviour. He was a self-taught man, even teaching himself the law. All his life, he enjoyed reading, learning, and poetry, common ninth house activities. Along with this, he would have been forming his own spiritual beliefs.

His south node was in Taurus. As a child and young man, he attended to his chores on the land; he did hands-on physical work and was paid for it, and he gave his pay to his father so the family could be fed. There is nothing more Taurean than this.

But as soon as he was able to leave home, he started on his own path and the passion of Scorpio took hold; he began to think for himself, to follow his own desires, to study subjects in-depth, and to reach for his own truth. There is no question that he believed deeply in his cause, and the more he inhabited the ninth house, the more intense and focused his beliefs became.

## 10. Look at the Relationship Houses

We look at the fifth and seventh houses for information about relationships. Neither of these houses have planets in them, and along with Abraham's moon in the twelfth house and his "me" sided chart, personal relationships were not of prime importance in his life.

The astrological sign in his seventh house was Leo, showing he would find fire-sign women attractive, and Venus being in Aries confirms this. His fifth house was in Gemini/Cancer. Gemini suggests a need to be able to talk with a lover, perhaps about his dreams, and the sign of Cancer in the house of children suggests a desire for a home-loving person to have his children.

His moon was unavailable to give emotionally. But it was in the sign of Capricorn, a traditional earth sign, so while he was disinterested in marriage (and maybe even love affairs), he was probably aware that should he have a traditional partnership. Capricorns desire to do things the way they have always been done; the continuance of the family line is incredibly important to them, so he might have desired children.

Although it is impossible to say what is in someone's heart, from these positions and signs it is likely he had no overwhelming desire for marriage but he accepted that tradition. If he ever thought about it (and we must assume it wasn't high on his priority list), he would have considered how advantageous it would be to make a financially astute liaison (Capricorn moon; Venus in second house of finances). He would have been drawn to a fire-sign woman who would have children and attend to the "others" side of the chart—be his go-between, in effect, and handle the day-to-day affairs of the household and family.

Mary Ann Todd, who later became Abraham's wife, was born December 13, 1818 at 6 p.m. in Lexington, Kentucky. She had a Cancer ascendant, which echoes Abraham's fifth house of children, and her moon was in Cancer, so she was ideally suited to the childbearing/mothering/nurturing role Abraham wanted in his wife. (She did go on to give him four sons.) She was also a very strong fire sign, having three planets in Sagittarius, and he sought a fire sign as a partner. She had three planets in Capricorn in her seventh house of marriage (Venus, Mercury, and Jupiter), which echo Abraham's moon in Capricorn, and her DC sign is Capricorn, suggesting he suited her image of a good marriage partner.

People who have "me" sided charts like Abraham find it hard to relate to people at a personal level and often choose heavily accented "other"-sided people. This is exactly what Mary was. Most of her planets are in the sixth and seventh houses. She was a very sociable, outgoing, active person, yet she was also strongly traditional with so many planets in Capricorn. She had an opposition line right across her chart, from AC to DC, showing a real fear of the bottom area, the collective community.

With all those planets in Capricorn, Mary would have looked to marry a man who would protect her from the collective community areas of life, and by the time she met Abraham he was already a renowned lawyer, so he was able to support her comfortably. Maybe she also foresaw he was destined for great things; fire signs are intuitive.

## 11. Look at the Career Houses

With no planets in the sixth house, Abraham was not drawn to hands-on physical labour. His childhood experiences of having to work hard on his family farm and being lent out to others by his father would have been well out of his comfort zone.

The tenth house, however, was a different matter. Saturn is the planet of structure and tradition; it likes things to stay the same, so it is clear Abraham had no desire to completely change the basic structures of society. It was his Neptune in the tenth house that made him an idealist. It gave him a compassionate love of his fellow man and a dislike of any inhumane act.

We looked at this Saturn/Neptune conjunction in the tenth house earlier, and combined with his free-thinking Aquarian sun and all those powerful planets in his first house, it seems Abraham was always destined for greatness.

☽ ✳ ☾

It is always best to have little or no knowledge about the individual you are doing a chart for because then you approach it without preconceived ideas and opinions. Never believe what you read or what you have heard. Let the chart reveal the truth.

This is a captivating chart because Abraham seems to have expressed all areas of his chart in the way he was meant to, astrologically speaking. We were able to see his weaknesses and fears and that he had self-doubts and concerns over the rightness of his actions. Isn't it nice to know even those in high and powerful positions are not as assured and confident as they seem?

It was also great that Abraham did some things because society expected it, like his marriage to Mary. In fact, like all of us, he was a flawed human being who simply did the best he could.

A chart is a way of looking deep into someone's soul. Many books have been written about Abraham, but in this one chart interpretation, it feels as though we got closer to the real man and his motivations.

# Thirteen
## SYNASTRY

*S*ynastry is also known as relationship astrology. It involves comparing two charts for any purpose, but generally for romantic possibilities between two people. However, if you are thinking of going into business with someone, this is a good tool for analysing possible problem areas before diving in and making a commitment. Use synastry for any questions involving two people to clarify strengths and weaknesses in the relationship.

### Interpreting a Birth Chart with Synastry

This chapter is included because it will give you good experience in understanding and interpreting charts. Without a doubt, you will be asked to compare two charts for a relationship—both for those who are already committed and for those who are considering it—so synastry is an important skill to master. It works for any close relationship, whether it is romantic, professional, or familial. In general, people who come for a relationship comparison are already emotionally involved, but it highlights problem areas, giving the individual insight and knowledge as to why these difficulties arise, and it can offer solutions for avoiding issues, solving them, and acceptance.

Most computer programs offer to display two charts on the screen, but it works best to print out both charts and work through each section bit by bit. For example, look at the elements in one chart, then the elements in the other, and compare as you go. Makes notes; otherwise you may have to go back and recheck. There is a lot of information in two charts!

Most sites also offer a single chart of the relationship. Once you understand how to compare two charts, you can move on to this if you want. A two-chart comparison seems more valid and informative, in my opinion, but that is for you to decide.

## 1. Count the Elements and the Motivations

This is the starting point. How many elements of fire, earth, air, and water do they have? What about cardinal, fixed, and mutable motivations? Do either of the partners have a dominant element?

If a person has a strong emphasis on one element, they may seek a partner who can balance and complement them—in effect, seeking what they lack in their partner. However, the one thing that drew them to the partner in the first place may eventually alienate them. For example, a predominantly earth person may marry a predominantly water type because they are looking to get in touch with some emotion and feeling, while the water type needs the stability of earth. Eventually, the earth person will likely feel overwhelmed by such deep emotion because they cannot understand it, and the water sign may pine away under the practical, phlegmatic approach of the earth person.

The elements occupied by the personal planets should be harmonious; each person should have at least one planet in the same elements as the other.

## 2. Compare the Ascendants

What sign is each person hiding behind? Ascendants that are square (three astrological signs apart) or in opposition to each other cause friction.

One example of a square is Aries-Cancer, so one partner with an Aries AC and the other with a Cancer AC are unlikely to be compatible. An opposition could be Cancer-Capricorn or Aries-Libra. Signs that are next to each other, like Libra and Scorpio, for example, often feel uncomfortable too.

A square in synastry causes tension and is not positive energy. However, if one person has a personal planet in the other's AC sign, this will negate any tension from squares or oppositions.

### 3. Look at the Relationship Houses

In both charts, look at the sign on the DC, the descendant/seventh house. Analyse what sort of person each wants based on the astrological sign on their DC.

Are there any planets in the seventh house? Are each partner's requirements matched by the other's chart?

Then look at the fifth house. Based on the sign and any planets in the fifth house, are they prone to affairs? What is their attitude toward having children? Does it seem like the partners have compatible tendencies?

### 4. Are There Any Planets on the AC, IC, DC, or MC?

When one person's sun or moon is in the other's first house, it is considered a karmic relationship. It is viewed by astrologers as a past-life connection. There is often an instant and very strong attraction between them. Both have a feeling that they already know this person, and linking up is natural and easy. And indeed, these two people often have some sort of continuing issue to resolve by being together. Relationships like this rarely end in a painful, destructive way. Generally, the lessons learned are positive, and the individuals come away with a sense of acceptance. Sometimes these relationships last a lifetime, but not always; there would need to be other harmonious links in their charts.

But any of the personal planets (especially Venus or Jupiter) on the other's AC, IC, DC, or MC (or in those houses) will have an especially deep impact. They may not be karmic, but these two people will instantly recognise each other as being someone special. The closer to the actual angle, the stronger the effect will be felt.

Note: People who marry for security rather than love often choose someone whose sun is in the same sign or element as their IC.

### 5. Check the Houses the Planets Fall In

What house is being activated by one of the other person's personal planets?

Start with the sun. For example, if one person's sun falls in the other's second house, it will activate that area when they are together, making them keen to build a firm financial foundation. If it is in the tenth, they may work together or start a business venture. Use the knowledge you've gained to analyse how you think these positions will affect the relationship.

Work through all of the planets. Where is the moon in each person's chart? If your moon is in their third house, it will make communication between you more emotional and nuanced. In the second, you feel emotionally secure as a couple, since the second house is ruled by Taurus. A list of what every planet means is a book in itself, so if you get stuck, just look it up on your phone. Information abounds. But have a go first at trying to analyse its likely impact. It takes a long time to learn so much, so be kind to yourself. Take a guess, then check to make sure you've got it right.

Especially look for personal planets in these houses: the first (because they will understand you), the fourth (because you both will want to set up home together), the fifth (because this is the house of self-expression, so they will encourage you to be you, and because it is the area of fun and children, so it is good to activate this house when together), and the seventh (because this is the long-term relationship house), as any link—apart from Saturn—is generally positive to the relationship.

## 6. Are Any of Their Planets Conjunct Each Other?

This is a very strong link, usually karmic, and both planets will be activated. If one's Mars is conjunct the other's sun, for example, the Mars person will motivate the other to be all they can be.

It isn't necessary to analyse each conjunction in detail; just be aware that most close contacts are beneficial. The exceptions are the outer planets. Saturn will suppress the planet that it is close to. Uranus will make the partner's planet more unpredictable. Neptune will cloud the issue connected with the planet it is next to. For example, if one partner's Neptune is conjunct the other's Mercury, there will be a dreamy aspect to their conversations that will hamper logical thoughts and plans. When on their own, they might be organised and clearheaded, but when together, the couple never seems to be able to come to any decisions. Pluto will try and control any close planet *and* the house in which it falls, so this could mean a subtle undercurrent of conflict.

## 7. Look at Other Aspects between Personal Planets

Difficult aspects like the square and opposition are going to cause problems. Mercury square Mercury will cause endless arguments—or certainly a different way of looking at things—even if there is deep love; in opposition, these people will think entirely differently. If one partner's moon is in opposition to the other's, they will feel so different that it will be difficult for them to understand each other.

Note that at the end of this chapter, there is a guide to how the aspects work between planets in synastry.

## 8. Where Is Saturn in Each of the Charts?

What sign is Saturn in? Which house is it in? Look at both charts. Saturn's placement is important because it will suppress the house it is in, as well as any planet that is within three degrees (conjunction).

If one partner has Saturn in the second house, it will make them careful (or mean) with money. If the other partner loves spending (Jupiter in the second or the sign of Leo in the second house with a personal planet there), this is obviously a future trouble spot. If it falls in the third, it will make the partner feel constrained when expressing opinions. In the fifth house, it will suppress the partner's self-expression, and so on.

Finally, look at any aspects involving Saturn. A red aspect from one person's Saturn to the other's Venus will affect the Venus partner's ability to give love. If Saturn is conjunct or in opposition to Mars, the Mars person will feel unable to do everything they wish to.

Positive aspects with Saturn still feel a bit uncomfortable, but generally there is a teaching and learning component. The Saturn partner will be exerting a subtle influence over the other planet in order to make it more productive.

## 9. Check the Outer Planets

Where is Uranus? In which area is each person unpredictable and unreliable, and where does it fall in the other's chart? Which area is it likely to disrupt when they are together?

Where is Neptune? Which area is likely to be dreamy/confusing when they are together? If one partner's Neptune falls in the other's second house, finances get confusing. In the third, communication is the issue.

Pluto wants to control. In which area, both separately and together, do they want control, and how will the other feel about this?

## 10. Look at the Quadrant Emphasis

Is one person needy? In other words, are all their planets on the "others" right-hand side with a strong seventh house? If so, will the other partner cope with this dependency? It is unlikely an air sign person would be happy with that, but a water sign person might like it.

Is one partner mostly at the top of the chart and the other at the bottom? This will mean one likes going out at night to socialise but the other might want to stay home to read or learn something.

Is one partner mostly on the left "me" side? If the other partner has more planets on the "others" side, they will be forced to take a lot of the responsibility for the day-to-day running of household affairs, as "me"-sided people prefer going off on their own to another room to quietly read or use the computer or listen to music.

## 11. Where Are the North and South Nodes?

Where is each person's comfort area (south node)? If one seeks solitude (south node in ninth or twelfth house) and the other loves being out socialising (south node in fifth house), there are bound to be compromises required.

Also, are their life directions compatible? For example, if one partner has the north node in the first house, this does not bode well for the relationship as this person is meant to be learning to live without a relationship!

Uncannily, very often the north node directions are productive to each other, especially in a karmic relationship. For example, if someone is moving from the sixth to the twelfth (which means moving away from hard work to a more meditative life), their partner may be a fourth house node person who is learning to put family above career, and who will eventually become the person who deals with the home, leaving the twelfth house person space to simply be.

Often the north node is reached later in life (unless there are personal planets in that house), so these changes and balances in a relationship are arrived at gradually and without conscious effort. They evolve. But it is a useful tool for understanding a person's life direction and where they actually feel more comfortable.

☽ ✳ ☾

Next we are going to talk about aspect lines between planets in a synastry chart.

## Aspects between Planets in Synastry

Aspects to the *angles* are not used in this book. This means an aspect between a planet and the AC, IC, DC, and MC, which are actually the start of houses. Although a lot of astrologers still do use aspects to angles, this is a more traditional (as in old) approach, and nowadays astrologers tend to only use links between the planets and not other parts of the chart.

Think of the chart as the layers of an onion, with each section being one layer. The houses are one layer, the astrological signs another, the planets a third. Keep each layer separate. The angles are important parts of the houses and the planets are a separate layer. If there is a planet that happens to be on an angle, then of course there will be an aspect going to that planet from another, but not to the angle itself.

The aspects we will be looking at here are the obvious, strong links between the planets themselves. These aspects are the ones you know: the square, opposition, sextile, trine, semi-sextile, and quincunx.

As a beginner, just start with the obvious aspects. Is your sun in direct opposition to your partner's? Is there a square between them? Refer back to chapter 6 to remind yourself how many signs apart these aspects need to be. An opposition is six signs apart, and square is three signs apart, remember? But the two planets themselves need to be fairly close by degrees. For example, if your sun is six degrees, your partner's sun would have to be quite close to that, say three degrees to nine degrees. So, if your sun is six degrees Aries and your partner's is three degrees Libra, it would make an opposition. If their sun was four degrees Gemini, it would form a square.

Astrologers use a fluid judgment when it comes to how many degrees to use. Some believe the sun's energy can extend up to ten degrees, but it's best to keep all the numbers as close as possible to be sure; the closer the number, the more intense the aspect.

## Sun

This is obviously a very important planet, so links to it from the partner's planets will have a significant impact on the relationship.

### SUN–SUN

Overall, aspects between suns are very positive. The only real problem is the square aspect, because both partners will be at loggerheads over their joint life direction.

An opposition can be a case of the attraction of opposites, and this can work well as long as there are other harmonious links. Suns can work in opposition because each partner will usually have an individual working life apart from the other, so they can express themselves outside of the relationship.

### SUN–MOON

Having an aspect line between one's sun and the other's moon is a necessity for a long-term relationship. The sextile and trine work well. If there is no contact, it helps if the planets share the same element or are at least in compatible signs.

### SUN ASPECTS TO MERCURY/VENUS/MARS

All good, except the square and sometimes the opposition. Sun–Venus is particularly helpful, but sun–Mars aspects can be too powerful and create competition between partners, especially the opposition and square, although the easier aspects can indicate good sexual compatibility.

### SUN–URANUS

The sun individual will think the Uranus partner has great charisma. Initially very exciting, but the unpredictability of Uranus may make the union short unless there are more stable aspects between them.

### SUN–NEPTUNE

The sun individual is fascinated by the Neptune partner, who supports, inspires, and empathises with the sun person. This could mean a spiritual union, but be aware that Neptune confuses and deceives, so it could end in the Neptune person letting the sun person down.

### SUN–PLUTO

Pluto contacts are always intense. The sun person may find themselves being transformed by the relationship; there will be much inner and outer growth. Beware, though, of power struggles and the desire of the Pluto person to dominate the sun person. The sun won't allow it, but it could mean endless interplay between them—and not all of it aboveboard from Pluto!

## Moon

Aspects between the moon are extremely important. It's likely negative aspects would have prevented the union from even starting, because the moon person would have felt misunderstood or railroaded as soon as they met. As the moon indicates our need to feel nurtured, someone who treads all over our sensitivities won't be accepted as our partner (and quite rightly!).

### MOON–MOON

Any harmonious link is great, but the opposition is unlikely to work. While suns in opposition can externalise conflict, moons in opposition are too emotional to do so. The opposition means neither partner will really feel at home with the other.

Conjunct moons or moons in the same sign are perfect placements. This often denotes a karmic link; perhaps the individuals met in past incarnations? There is a great bond and understanding between them. Moons in the same element likewise share a common bond.

### MOON–MERCURY

The square and semi-sextile aspects can cause problems. The Mercury person will have little regard for the feelings of the moon person, resulting in the moon person feeling insecure, nervous, and unloved. There could be verbal criticism from the Mercury person, especially of the other's feelings. Other aspects work well.

### MOON–VENUS

Perfect! Even in the difficult aspects.

### MOON–MARS

Sexual attraction will abound with positive aspects, but the square and the opposition might provoke arguments. The Mars person might run roughshod over the moon person's feelings by ignoring them or trying to dominate them.

### MOON–URANUS

Sexual attraction. The Uranus person will stimulate the moon person to have new feelings and experiences, but this might prove too disruptive and unreliable for the moon person to cope with.

### MOON–PLUTO

The Pluto person can touch the moon person deeply; this is either transformative or traumatic. This opposition is dangerous, as the Pluto person could be emotionally manipulative.

## Mercury

Conversation is vital to positive long-term relationships, so aspects to Mercury are of great importance. It is unlikely a couple would get together in the first place if their Mercury signs weren't harmonious, but I have known relationships where Mercury signs were square and humor was used to deflate tension. Each relationship is unique, and it is for the people involved to decide how much they are willing to tolerate and where they draw the line— and, indeed, how to resolve difficult aspects when the rest of the relationship is really good.

### MERCURY–ALL PERSONAL PLANETS

Communication is very important in relationships. All harmonious links between Mercury and the other planets is beneficial, but the squares and oppositions are difficult. The square indicates arguments, whereas the oppositions indicate a completely different mental approach.

### MERCURY–URANUS

Positive aspects indicate telepathic understanding and mental stimulation between the partners, but the difficult aspects will not work because they create extreme differences in views and opinions.

### MERCURY–PLUTO

Squares, oppositions, quincunx, and conjunctions are difficult to handle. The Pluto person may force their opinion on the Mercury person or subtly manipulate their thinking processes. This could indicate mental cruelty.

Positive aspects indicate that the Pluto person will encourage the Mercury person to expand their mind and to think in a deeper way.

## Venus

Being the planet of love, aspects to Venus are paramount in creating a loving, harmonious relationship. Even those aspects considered negative—the opposition and square—are softened when linked to Venus.

### VENUS–MARS

Most aspects between Venus and other planets are beneficial. Venus and Mars indicate a good sexual relationship, and unlike any other planets, the square and opposition only serve to heighten the sexual attraction between them.

### VENUS–URANUS

Aspects between Uranus and Venus stimulate the relationship, providing excitement and change. There is often something unusual about this partnership.

Difficult aspects might mean the Uranus partner is unfaithful or won't be tied down by the relationship.

### VENUS–PLUTO

These aspects could work either way; they could raise the relationship to great heights or gradually destroy it. Harmonious links mean a deep, fulfilling relationship, with the Venus person discovering new depths to love. Difficult links can mean considerable cruelty or trauma, usually brought on in a subtle way by Pluto, which may be possessive or manipulative of gentle Venus.

Whatever the link, sex is a driving force, but negative links might mean Pluto forces demands on Venus that aren't acceptable.

### VENUS–NEPTUNE

Positive links create a sensitive, inspiring, romantic union. Neptune might willingly self-sacrifice for Venus.

The square and opposition might mean the Neptune person misleads or deceives the Venus person.

## Mars

Being aggressive by nature, Mars can stimulate a good sex drive, but in square or opposition to the other's personal planets, it might be too disruptive.

### MARS–URANUS

Not favourable. Squares and oppositions can end up in outright rebellion, resulting in many and frequent separations. Usually, though, the partners have a strong draw to return each other. Sometimes they just need to be apart for a while. Certainly not a calm relationship, but some people like a bit of drama!

### MARS–NEPTUNE

Negative aspects are not easy. Neptune has a way of undermining Mars, making the Mars person lose drive and direction. Positive links can work well if the Neptune person supports and encourages the Mars person to greater achievement.

### MARS–PLUTO

Pluto can feel threatened by Mars, so Pluto will try to control it. Mars naturally rebels! There are bound to be arguments. With harmonious links, there is a good and exciting bond.

## Jupiter

All contacts are generally good, though be aware that the Jupiter partner may make any planet it activates in the other's chart act in a larger-than-life way. For example, contacts between Jupiter and the moon will heighten emotions. Contacts between Jupiter and Mars might make ambitions a bit unrealistic.

## Saturn

Knowing what we do about Saturn, it is easy to surmise the effect of one partner's Saturn on the other's personal planets. Good aspects (trine and sextile) indicate a teaching aspect to the relationship. Difficult aspects mean outright suppression of a planet by Saturn. It is doubtful a relationship with one partner's Saturn sitting on the other's sun, moon, Venus, Mercury, or Mars will work long-term, as the non-Saturn planet will not be able to function effectively.

## Uranus

Uranus disrupts and creates havoc, so any planet it comes into contact with will suddenly act in an unpredictable way. The Uranus partner may make the other feel more alive and free—or just insecure. It depends on the rest of their charts and which planets are affected. Sometimes the Uranus partner will demand a more open relationship. Whether this will be acceptable is dependent on the other person's entire chart. Generally, aspects involving Uranus mean the relationship is short-lived but exciting.

## Neptune

Neptune contacts add a dreamy feel to any planet it has links to. Sometimes the Neptune partner can prove unreliable. As previously mentioned, it can muddy the waters and create confusion, especially when in aspects to Mercury. Think Mercury in Pisces!

## Pluto

Pluto wants to control, so any planet in close contact will be subject to manipulation. If it is the moon or Mercury, beware. The Pluto person will try and control the emotions or communication of their partner. ("You talk too much," "You don't know what you are talking about," etc.)

With a Pluto–Pluto aspect, a conjunction or opposition will create a dramatic fight for control. Exciting but exhausting! The square will create angry confrontation that is hidden from view.

Having no aspect to Pluto is preferable. Even better if it sits in an area of the partner's chart (house) where it won't do any harm, or where the other person will happily hand control to the Pluto person. Sometimes we like others to take charge of certain areas.

$$\text{☽ ✳ ☾}$$

Synastry aspects are often very subtle because they are only felt by the people involved. Be aware, too, that one man's meat is another's poison; in other words, what one person can tolerate or accept, someone else might find intolerable. As before, never make any judgment or comment because we are all looking for different things from our relationships based on our own upbringing, personality, and strengths and weaknesses. You may feel someone you know is being controlled by a Pluto-type person, but perhaps they just like letting someone else be in control? It is not for an astrologer to judge or pass comment.

# CONCLUSION

You now have all the tools that you need to interpret birth charts. From here on out, it is simply experience. Practise, practise, practise on as many charts as you can get your hands on! It will be easier than you think, as most people jump at the chance to have someone interpret their chart, even those who profess disinterest. Astrology is a vast subject, so delve deeper by reading all about the aspects that interest you most.

We all start somewhere. Hopefully, this is your new beginning. Happy chart reading!